CW00500720

COLLECTED POEMS AND

CHARLOTTE MEW was born in London in 1869, the third child of an architect, and was educated at a girls' school in London. Her first published work was a short story in *The Yellow Book* in 1894. In May 1912 she was introduced to May Sinclair, a leading novelist who was active in the women's suffrage movement. Mew fell in love with her, but although Sinclair encouraged her writing, she did not reciprocate Mew's feelings and the relationship eventually broke up. The period from 1913 was one of the most productive periods for Mew's poetry, however, and she became an increasingly published and admired poet. Living with her mother and sister Anne, an artist, in difficult circumstances, she found freedom and inspiration on holidays in France and Belgium. In 1923 she was awarded a Civil List pension on the recommendation of John Masefield, Walter de la Mare and Thomas Hardy. A fear of hereditary mental illness had led Mew and her sister to vow not to marry: both her elder brother and another younger sister had been taken to mental hospitals. In 1927, still grieving from the death of her sister, Mew killed herself, possibly because she feared the onset of insanity.

VAL WARNER has worked as a teacher, editor and writer. She was Creative Writing Fellow at the University College of Swansea and Writer in Residence at the University of Dundee, and has received a Gregory Award. Her publications include the pamphlet *These Yellow Photos* (1971), *Under the Penthouse* (1973) *Before Lunch* (1986) and *The Centenary Corbière* (translations of Tristan Corbière, 1975).

Fyfield*Books* aim to make available some of the great classics of British and European literature in clear, affordable formats, and to restore often neglected writers to their place in literary tradition.

Fyfield*Books* take their name from the Fyfield elm in Matthew Arnold's 'Scholar Gypsy' and 'Thyrsis'. The tree stood not far from the village where the series was originally devised in 1971.

Roam on! The light we sought is shining still.
Dost thou ask proof? Our tree yet crowns the hill,
Our Scholar travels yet the loved hill-side

from 'Thyrsis'

CHARLOTTE MEW

Collected Poems and Selected Prose

Edited with an introduction by
VAL WARNER

FyfieldBooks

CARCANET

First published in Great Britain in 1997 by
Carcanet Press Limited
Alliance House
Cross Street
Manchester M2 7AQ

This impression 2003

A CIP catalogue record for this book is available from the British Library
ISBN 1 85754 706 3

The publisher acknowledges financial assistance from
the Arts Council of England

Funded by THE ARTS COUNCIL OF ENGLAND

Printed and bound in England by SRP Ltd, Exeter

Contents

The Rambling Sailor (1929)

Early poems printed at the end
of *The Rambling Sailor*

Poems collected or published posthumously

SELECTED PROSE
Stories

Essay

Play

Acknowledgements

In connection with material in the Introduction, I should like to thank the British Museum Central Archives Secretariat, Jill Farringdon, Michael Farringdon, the Hogarth Press, Francis King, Sue Lowe and staff at the British Library, the National Art Library, the National Library of Scotland and the University of Reading Library.

I consulted census returns at the Public Record Office, electoral registers at Camden Local Studies and Archives Centre, Holborn Library, and documents from Somerset House and St Catherine's House.

The Introduction also draws on material used when preparing my *Collected Poems & Prose of Charlotte Mew*, including that from the major collections of Mew papers in the Berg Collection of the New York Public Library; the Poetry Collection, the Lockwood Memorial Library, the University of Buffalo; and the British Library.

Introduction

Charlotte Mary Mew was born in London on 15 November 1869, the third child of Frederick Mew (1832-98) from the Isle of Wight. His family ran Newport's best-known inn, The Bugle – as The Bull, it was the Parliamentary Commissioners' base at the so-called Treaty of Newport in the Civil War – and a farm where he grew up. Frederick Mew was sent to Mr Wotton's School in London and became an architect, in 1863 marrying the daughter of his well-known partner, H.E. Kendall the younger. Anna Maria Mardon Kendall (1837-1923), whose aunt married into the 'royal' builders, the Cubitts, apparently felt that she herself had married beneath her. Of the seven Mew children, two sons died after a few months, and a third aged five.

Charlotte was born at 30 Doughty Street, Mecklenburgh Square, where the family lived till 1890 (not 1888, according to the electoral roll). They then moved up-market to 9 Gordon Street, Gordon Square, Bloomsbury, where Charlotte lived till 1922. The essay 'An Old Servant', about her nanny, describes the Mew nursery. The children went to the Isle of Wight farm for summer holidays.

'Lotti' attended the Lucy Harrison School for Girls in Gower Street, part of the time boarding with two other pupils in the Hampstead house of the headmistress, Lucy Harrison, editor of *Spenser for Home and School,* 1883 (not, as has been stated, the author of *Conversational Lessons on Social Geography for Teachers of Infants*). Possibly this was because Charlotte was disobedient at home, as a cousin hinted. There was a story of Fred Mew on his knees to Harrison, pleading for Charlotte to stay in the school. Charlotte later referred to staying with old aunts she disliked in Somerset. But for Miss Harrison she developed a schoolgirl 'crush', banging her head against the wall when she heard that the headmistress was leaving.

Charlotte apparently learnt only what interested her – English literature, and a little about art and music. She played the organ and the piano. In 1891, she obtained a ticket for the British Museum Reading Room.

Charlotte's favourite cousin related that in the early 1890s

Charlotte 'kept company' with Sam Chick, brother of old school-friends. On Census night 1891, Charlotte was staying with the Chicks, though Sam was away. In 1899, his sister Mary and his affluent father, a lace-manufacturer, witnessed Mrs Mew's will. Charlotte's 1890s' short stories mostly focus on a fatal wedding.

'An Old Servant' mentions 'sheets of pathetically laboured MSS' in the Mew nursery. When she left the Gower Street school, Charlotte's sister Anne (1873-1927) attended the Royal Female School of Art (later merged in the Central) and the sisters acquired more artistic friends. Charlotte smoked, swore and visited unchaperoned – and was noted for embroidery.

In 1894 Henry Harland, literary editor of *The Yellow Book* of which Aubrey Beardsley was art editor, published Mew's story 'Passed' in the second issue – an impressive début. Ella D'Arcy, another contributor, listed Charlotte Mew among literati such as Kenneth Grahame, Max Beerbohm, George Moore, Arthur Symons, Evelyn Sharp, Netta Syrett and occasionally Edmund Gosse and Henry James at Harland's Saturday evening At Homes in his Cromwell Road flat. Harland suggested that the magazine's publishers, John Lane and Elkin Mathews, might publish a volume of her stories; Mew seems not to have pursued this, perhaps because she then had insufficient stories.

Although Mew seems not to have appeared in print again for five years, she continued writing short stories. One of her unpublished stories, 'A Wedding Day', is dated 1895, and 'An Open Door', published in *Temple Bar* in 1903, was rejected by *Black-wood's* in 1898 after earlier encouragement to submit further stories. On stylistic grounds, most of her prose unpublished till the *Collected* edition of 1981 may be ascribed to this period. In 1899, she placed 'The China Bowl' with *Temple Bar*, which thenceforward till 1905 published her stories, articles and – from 1901 – poems.

There have been doubts over Mew's authorship of two 'V. R. I.' sonnets printed anonymously in *Temple Bar*, March 1901, following Queen Victoria's death; letters to the printer in the archive of *Temple Bar*'s then-publisher, Macmillan, deposited in the British Library in 1982, confirm it. (Contrary to some scholars' statements, Mew did not contribute pseudonymously to *The Yellow Book* as Charles Catty – poet and bank official.)

Mew's article 'Notes in a Brittany Convent' and the linked poem 'The Little Portress' resulted from a visit to Brittany in 1901, in a party of six women staying at the convent of St Gilda de Rhuys, apparently the first of her visits to France and Belgium before World War I.

In 1982, Marjorie Watts's article confirmed Charlotte Mew's lesbianism – though many readers would have had little doubt, given her writing's romantic focus on women. Female homosexuality was never illegal – though it almost became so in the 1921 Act – but in the climate of the day, sharpened by the Wilde trial of 1895, discretion would have been absolute. It may be that we know nothing of the most important relationship/s in Charlotte's life. With almost one in three late Victorian women a spinster, a range of female relationships flourished. Charlotte probably heard that Amy Greener, the successor to her former headmistress Lucy Harrison, moved to York to teach under Harrison as headmistress of the Quaker School, The Mount, and live with her in retirement till Lucy's death. Radclyffe Hall's *The Unlit Lamp* (1924), published four years before her prosecuted *Well of Loneliness*, showed passionate friendships between female musicians in 1890s' London.

In *Yellow Book* days, Charlotte was perhaps attracted to Ella D'Arcy. She holidayed with friends in the Channel Islands in 1895, a year Ella spent much time there. Ella, notorious for male lovers including John Lane, moved to Paris in 1898. Charlotte met her there in April 1902; sentences in Charlotte's letter to Ethel Oliver, which biographer Penelope Fitzgerald considers revealing, as to Charlotte's intense feelings for Ella, could as well refer to family difficulties in England. In 1909 Ella wrote to Charlotte that she didn't know she was a poet.

The painter Kate (Katherine) Righton had a run of *Temple Bars* with Charlotte's work and was the only (because poorest?) friend (as opposed to relative) to benefit largely by Charlotte's will; is it significant that in Charlotte's story 'Mark Stafford's Wife', published in *Temple Bar* in January 1905, Kate (Katharine) Relton is loved by a man named Charlie? (Though not linked with her own, Charlotte used the name Ella in two stories and Stella in a third – dates of composition unknown.) According to rumour, Charlotte loved Beatrice Hastings, whose lovers included A.R.

Orage of *The New Age*, Modigliani and probably Katherine Mansfield.

In her 1953 Memoir, Alida Monro, a radical friend from 1915, married to a homosexual, wrote about Charlotte: 'She had a strict moral code in respect of other people's conduct, particularly in regard to their sex relationships, and absolutely cut out from her friendship anyone on whom a breath of scandal blew.' There is various evidence that Alida was aware of Charlotte's sexuality, which doubtless from loyalty to her she didn't clarify in her Memoir.

Charlotte's surviving letters, dating mainly from her later life – and her early poems 'V. R. I.' – suggest respect for social conventions. She didn't register to vote till 1923, though eligible in 1918. But her writing shows awareness of social inequalities, and she did voluntary work for both Miss Paget's Girls' Club and the War Pensions Committee.

Charlotte told Alida that hereditary insanity had led herself and her sister to vow not to marry. Her elder brother, Henry (1865-1901), had become schizophrenic and been taken away to Peckham House Lunatic Asylum, south London. Around the time of his death, her little sister Freda (1879-1958) was taken away to the Isle of Wight County Mental Hospital, Whitecroft, Newport. The Mew siblings were close, and Charlotte would have feared entering 'the asylum' herself, especially as her maternal uncle was 'simple'.

For Anne, probably heterosexual, this decision was a genuine burden. A painter who had at least seven pictures exhibited in London and Liverpool, Anne also worked at restoration for an antiques-dealer. She resembled Marie Antoinette and was considered the most mentally stable of the family, but suffered more physical ill-health than Charlotte, whose writing she encouraged.

In her youth, Charlotte had an Anglo-Catholic phase; Anne died an Anglo-Catholic. Charlotte's closest friends included Elsie O'Keeffe (*née* Millard), a Roman Catholic, and Ethel Oliver, a Quaker. Charlotte perhaps lost some Christian belief, though her letters show she sometimes attended Anglican and Roman Catholic services. Her work shows how 'God-bothered' she remained. Poem after poem polarizes God, invariably in the Second Person of the Christian Trinity, and a human lover. Because the human aspect of Christ is evoked, this clash reads almost as if between two people. The poems are resolved in a sense that Christ will understand or be ignored, as in 'Absence':

> But call, call, and though Christ stands
> Still with scarred hands
> Over my mouth, I must answer. So
> I will come – He shall let me go!

Mew's proposal to the publisher Elkin Mathews to edit Emily Brontë's poems was rejected, but in 1904 *Temple Bar* printed her essay 'The Poems of Emily Brontë'. Apart from a handful, Mew saw her poems 'in form and structure . . . curiously deficient', yet sublime 'in their simple but compelling passion'. Mew identified strongly with 'this love-song of a woman who never loved'. Possibly, Charlotte died a virgin – though her writing suggests sexual experience.

As the only outlet for her poems and for all but three of her stories, the collapse of *Temple Bar* in 1906 must have been devastating for Mew. Apart from the poem 'Requiescat' in the *Nation* in 1909, she apparently published nothing until 'The Farmer's Bride' in the same weekly, February 1912. Emotional, sensuous, accessible, the farmer's monologue is her best known poem:

> Shy as a leveret, swift as he,
> Straight and slight as a young larch tree,
> Sweet as the first wild violets, she,
> To her wild self. But what to me?

In May 1912, Mew met 'Sappho' Catharine Amy Dawson Scott, a novelist who later founded International PEN and was then trying to establish a literary salon in Southall, the west London suburb where she lived with her doctor husband. Charlotte, who liked children, sometimes took her three children including the schoolgirl Marjorie (later Watts) to the zoo.

Next year, in her efforts to further Charlotte's career, Sappho (inappropriately nicknamed from the title of her first publication, a long poem) introduced her to May Sinclair. A leading novelist in Britain and America, Sinclair was active in women's suffrage, deeply interested in philosophy and psychology, and about to help establish the Medico-Psychological Clinic of London. Charlotte wrote her a letter about her newly-published novel *The Combined Maze*. May replied on 17 March 1913 and later read Mew's poems, stories and play *The China Bowl* (adapted from her short story), encouraging her and approaching editors on her behalf.

Spring 1913 to spring 1914 was Mew's *annus mirabilis* of poetry including 'Fame', 'The Quiet House', 'Ken', 'In Nunhead Cemetery' and 'The Forest Road'. 'The Fête' was written by Sinclair's method of withdrawal (in Mew's case, to Dieppe, on holiday alone), fired by erotic feeling for Sinclair, as soon became clear, and placed by Sinclair with Ezra Pound at the *Egoist*.

In 1970 May Sinclair's future biographer, Theophilus Boll, printed the novelist G.B. (Gladys 'Peter') Stern's somewhat farcical reference to an amorous Charlotte leaping after an unresponsive May over her bed. In 1982 Marjorie Watts, referring to her mother Sappho's unpublished journal for the early summer of 1914, confirmed Charlotte's advances. May, who perhaps renounced her love for a man when she was young, had by then long been established as a woman alone. May told Sappho and G.B. Stern that she did not like Charlotte's advances, but she remained a helpful friend, writing Charlotte in 1915 that if she could, she would have published her poetry herself.

Alida Klementaski (later Monro) had been 'electrified' by 'The Farmer's Bride' in the *Nation* in 1912 and memorized the poem. A year later, she met the Georgian poet Harold Monro who had opened the Poetry Bookshop in January 1913, planning to publish poetry, and went to work for him. Later, she repeated the poem to Monro; they wrote to Mew c/o the *Nation*, offering her a book on the strength of that one poem.

How little is known about even Charlotte's later life is highlighted by her remark about the forthcoming book in a letter to Harold Monro: unidentified 'friends who not so long ago would have taken a personal interest in it being no longer alive . . .'. Conceivably, Charlotte was referring to Lucy Harrison who died on 2 May 1915, though there is no record of any post-school contact. The unnamed dedicatee of *The Farmer's Bride* was probably her insane brother Henry, buried in Nunhead Cemetery, south London. 'In Nunhead Cemetery', though written from a male persona about a dead woman, draws on autobiography, as 'The Quiet House' transmutes the Mew family in the Gordon Street house.

The final poem 'Exspecto Resurrectionem', about a dead child, perhaps evokes Richard Cobham, the brother who died aged five when Charlotte was seven. Despite the doubts expressed in the penultimate poem 'Madeleine in Church', still unresolved in its final 'Or, if, for once, He would only speak', 'Exspecto Resurrectionem' and the dedication from Psalm 21 give the book a Christian frame.

Although sales were low, the book received at least ten reviews, including H.D.'s (Hilda Doolittle) in the *Egoist*, comparing Mew with Browning. When Harold Monro asked May Sinclair to approach reviewers or literary editors, she had already written to five, including H.D.

Both the Monros championed 'Aunty's work, later amply representing it in their anthologies. Asked by Edward Marsh, editor of the immensely popular *Georgian Poetry*, to suggest work by a woman for the third volume, Harold Monro argued for 'The Farmer's Bride' but Walter de la Mare vetoed it. No woman was included. In 1919 Marsh was again seeking a 'poetess' for *Georgian Poetry IV* and Monro again urged Mew, but Fredegond Shove was chosen.

Sydney Cockerell, Director of the Fitzwilliam Museum, Cambridge, and once secretary to William Morris, introduced himself to Mew after reading her book. A friendship developed between the Mew sisters and Cockerell and his wife Kate, an illustrator, that lasted until Charlotte's death. Her extensive correspondence with them portrays the last decade of her life, with outings to lectures and galleries – 'Bach is beyond me' – and the occasional weekend with friends in the country, and with the Cockerells themselves. He introduced Mew's poetry to many of his wide circle, including the poet Wilfred Scawen Blunt, T.E. Lawrence, and Dame Laurentia McLachlan, Abbess of Stanbrook, friend of

Bernard Shaw, and pioneer in the restoration of the Gregorian chant in England. In 1919 Cockerell brought Siegfried Sassoon to tea with Mew; Sassoon remained loyal to her work, writing in 1953 that she was 'the only poet who brought a lump to my throat'.

Cockerell told Mew that Hugh Walpole admired her poetry. So did the Poet Laureate, Robert Bridges, who was photographed with her at his house on Boar's Hill, outside Oxford. Lady Ottoline Morrell pursued her with invitations. Virginia Woolf considered *The Farmer's Bride* 'very good and interesting and unlike anyone else'. Dorothy Wellesley of the Woolfs' Hogarth Press later, in vain, invited Mew to submit a book for their Living Poets series.

Like Woolf, Thomas Hardy deemed Mew 'far and away the best living woman poet'. His regard probably meant most to Mew, who revered his work, a strong influence, not only in the use of dialect. After reading *The Farmer's Bride,* he invited her to visit at Max Gate. The visit was made in December 1918, and followed by at least one more visit. His second wife Florence and Charlotte became friends, meeting in London.

It is revealing that despite so much encouragement, after July 1914 Mew apparently published nothing in magazines during the war years, until July 1919. In 1915 she added the last stanzas of 'Madeleine in Church' and probably wrote the short story 'Spine', a far clumsier application of word-association technique than in her poems, and in the name Violet and its resonances echoing Sinclair's *Combined Maze.* Labelled by Mew 'The Gipsy' (*sic*) and partially copy-edited, the MS of this story was probably accepted 1915-16 by Henry Savage's *Yellow Book*ish *The Gypsy,* where Dorothy Richardson's soon-to-be husband, Alan Odle, was art editor – and was returned to Mew unpublished when the magazine collapsed. (Assessing Dorothy Richardson's fiction in 1918, Sinclair was the first to apply to literature the term 'stream of consciousness'.) Despite the contrived antithesis between the banker's gold and the corn's, the little story 'The Wheat', probably also written then (judging by its style), works better.

Notwithstanding May's continuing friendship, any dream of her love faded. May's letters to Charlotte trail off in late summer 1916, for no perceptible cause – but Charlotte may have destroyed later letters. (May did not keep Charlotte's letters, perhaps as Boll suggests to protect Charlotte from her 'indiscretion'.) After May told her about the 'bed-leaping' episode, Sappho Dawson-Scott dropped Charlotte temporarily ('pervert' declared her journal); invited by Sappho to read her poems in 1917 at her Tomorrow Club for new writers, Charlotte refused. Perhaps Charlotte broke with May because she resented her talking about her with her friends. Certainly, she owed May much: only the Monros did more for her work. Given the theme of mental illness in Mew's poems, it was at least careless that in *Mary Oliver* (1919), Sinclair named a mad character Charlotte; in her next novel *The Romantic* (1920), the main female character is – compensatingly? – named Charlotte.

In 1921 a new edition of *The Farmer's Bride* added eleven more poems to the original seventeen, but most were short and some had been written before the 1916 edition. Macmillan published it in America as *Saturday Market*.

When the lease of the Gordon Street house expired in 1922, the Mew sisters rented the upper part of 86 Delancey Street, near Regent's Park. Mrs Mew was reported as very preoccupied with keeping up appearances – as was Charlotte. After Mr Mew's death from cancer in 1898, lodgers had become a financial necessity. Women from middle-class Victorian families would not normally have earned their own living, and until Fred Mew's death finances appeared sound, despite the secret drain of care for Henry (and later Freda). While only the top floors were let in the Gordon Street house, this was kept almost as secret as the insane relatives. 'Ma' died in May 1923. Charlotte asked Anne to write Cockerell with the news; presumably she herself was too upset. A letter from Cockerell, November 1923, apparently refers to her suicide attempt with bleach, presaging the aftermath of Anne's death . . .

In December 1923 Mew was awarded a Civil List pension of £75 a year, on the recommendation of John Masefield, Walter de la Mare – despite his earlier reservations about her work – and Thomas Hardy.

In 1926 she was working on 'Aglaë', a long short story (or novel?), which she marked 'abandoned, October 1926'. Anne was unwell and Charlotte gave up the Delancey Street lease. When they returned to London after some weeks in Chichester in autumn 1926, Anne's studio in the Hogarth Studios, 64 Charlotte Street W.1, became their home. Anne died of cancer in June 1927. Alida Monro called Charlotte 'inconsolable'. Yet she still pursued an intellectual life, as her final renewal of her B.M. Reading Room ticket in July 1927 shows.

Anne left Charlotte her whole estate, net value £3,510 – £85,000 in 1996 terms – indicating that the Mews were better-off than believed. (Some of Anne's medical bills were paid by Edward T. Browne, a marine biologist with a private income and husband (not father) of the sisters' friend, Maggie; Anne painted Edward's portrait, exhibited at the Royal Academy in 1919.)

On 15 February 1928, Charlotte went into a nursing-home at 37 Beaumont Street W.1 for treatment for neurasthenia. On 24 March, two days after the anniversary of her brother Henry's death in 1901, she killed herself there by drinking half a bottle of the disinfectant lysol, which she had walked out a few minutes earlier to buy. The coroner's verdict was 'suicide whilst of unsound mind'. Probably, she resolved to die because she feared signs of insanity were emerging. (Inconsistencies in her life may be related to an irrational streak, which friends noticed.) Certainly, it was not to 'prove' she was a poet, as Germaine Greer has argued.

The next year, the Poetry Bookshop reissued the enlarged *Farmer's Bride* and published *The Rambling Sailor;* Alida Monro pointed out that many of the latter poems had also been written before 1916. Mew's later admirers included Rose Macaulay, Dylan Thomas and the New Zealand novelist Margaret Escott.

Charlotte Mew's strength is the monologue, dramatic or interior, which she was already using in 'An Ending': her friends the Chicks dated their MS copy to the early 1890s:

> You know that road beside the sea,
>   Walled by the wavin' wheat,
> Which winds down to the little town,
>   Wind-blown and grey and up the crooked street?

We'd used to meet
Just at the top, and when the grass was trodden down
'Twas by our feet.

Her other earlier work, mainly in regular metre, includes a number of sonnets yet 'An Ending', with lines of different numbers of iambs, reveals how early Mew was evolving the metrical technique of her major poems twenty years later. Their rhyming free verse often includes lines of different numbers of iambs. Mew had a strong natural sense of rhythm, also revealed in her piano-playing and youthful fondness for dancing.

Sometimes regarded as Georgian for her poems set in the English countryside, at her most sentimental over nuns and prostitutes Mew sounds very '1890s'. Yet, her techniques including rhymed free verse are modernist – and very early. Pound, who published her long poem 'The Fête' in the *Egoist* in 1914, did not arrive in London till 1908, with copies of his first, self-published book *A Lume Spento*, ambitious to re-vivify English poetry. D.H. Lawrence's poems were first published by Ford Madox Ford in the *English Review* in 1909. Possibly, Mew was prompted by the work of these poets to develop her radical poetic forms of twenty years earlier.

Like T.S. Eliot, Mew might have been influenced by Laforgue's rhyming free verse, publicized in England from 1908 by F.S. Flint, or earlier by Matthew Arnold's 'Dover Beach' or Milton's – unrhymed – *Samson Agonistes*. She admired Whitman, who perhaps influenced 'The Forest Road', unrhymed like 'Moorland Night'.

The anthologized Mew, for instance in Philip Larkin's *Oxford Book of Twentieth-century English Verse* (1973), is the Georgian Mew – if only on grounds of length. Her most experimental poems are her longest, written in her *annus mirabilis* from spring 1913, possibly structurally influenced by May Sinclair. Even sympathetic critics like Edith Sitwell criticized lapses into obscurity and, in Edgell Rickword's phrase, 'her tendency to become conversational with an indeterminate you'. There is also their 'rawness', amounting to an extreme subjectiveness without irony, unlike the Eliot of 'Prufrock' and 'Portrait of a Lady', almost exactly contemporary; May Sinclair perceptively compared Mew with D.H. Lawrence. 'The Circus Clown', E.V. Knox's brilliant albeit unrhymed parody, caught her solemn subjectivity:

> I wonder why it was you made me smile.
> I think because you had a funny face,
> White as the moonlight, and a red red nose,
> And the moon dripped upon the floor like this
> Two years ago. The floor looked just the same.
> *There is something very terrible about a floor.*
>
> And then the fête . . .

Though Mew loathed it, inclusion in Knox's 1921 *Punch* series was a tribute. Most readers would surely be carried by the passion of her unique experimental poems.

Perhaps placing the story 'Passed' in *The Yellow Book*, 1894, led Mew through the 1890s to concentrate on prose, in which she never developed the original voice that she had in poetry. Though her characters generally convince, her early stories, focusing on heightened moments, often look as if they should be poems. Her later short stories are more crafted but, like all her prose, too obviously influenced. To May Sinclair's identification of the influence of Henry James and Henry Harland could be added Hardy, Poe, the Wilde of *A Portrait of Dorian Grey* and Zola. Possibly Mew influenced Sinclair: compare the colour imagery of the red flowers in *Harriett Frean* (1922) and Mew's 'Quiet House', 1913.

Throughout her writing, Mew focuses on women – either women who are themselves objects of passion or romance, using as personae frequently colourless male narrators, or women who crave passion, introducing nondescript male love-objects for them.

In Mew's concern to articulate physical passion, which is always shown negated, the monologue, dramatic or interior, is a *cri de coeur*, like her third-person prose descriptions of her protagonists' most intense feelings. Negation is by the living death of the loss of youth, by death itself, by the workings of a malign fate, by the dictates of conventional morality, by renunciation and even

– in her essay on Emily Brontë and the story 'Elinor', perhaps a fictionalized Emily – by the glorification of the renunciation of all love into itself a kind of passion. Of Brontë, Mew wrote: 'Never perhaps has passion been portrayed as she portrayed it – wayward and wild as storm [. . .] And nature is presented to us by the same unerring hand.' Mew's juxtaposition of passion and Brontë's treatment of nature is fundamental.

The theme of natural beauty, present throughout Mew's work, strengthens later. In 'In the Fields' and 'Old Shepherd's Prayer', the reality of this world's beauty contrasts with the Christian promise of the after-life. In the pair of war poems 'May, 1915' and 'June, 1915', omitted from many First World War anthologies, she uses nature as touchstone for the abiding – in her pre-Hiroshima and less polluted world. A peacetime counterpart is the dying banker's understanding in 'The Wheat'. While in 'Moorland Night':

> Over my head the curlews call,
> And now there is the night wind in my hair;
> My heart is against the grass and the sweet earth . . .

A Note on the Text

This edition, including all Charlotte Mew's known poems, follows the 1921 edition of *The Farmer's Bride* 'with eleven new poems', and *The Rambling Sailor*, 1929. Of the poems uncollected until my *Collected Poems & Prose* (Carcanet, 1981), 'To a Little Child in Death' was first published in *Temple Bar*, CXXIV, September 1901, and 'Péri en mer' in *The Englishwoman*, XX, 59, November 1913; 'V.R.I.' was first published anonymously in *Temple Bar*, CXXII, March 1901; the typescripts of 'An Ending', 'A Question', 'Left Behind', 'A Farewell' and '"There shall be no night there"' are in the Frederick B. Adams Collection and were first printed by Mary C. Davidow in 'Charlotte Mew: Biography and Criticism' (unpublished Ph.D. thesis, 1960, Brown University, USA).

The story 'Elinor', whose typescript is in the British Library (Additional MSS. 57754), was apparently unpublished until the 1981 *Collected*. 'The Minnow Fishers' was listed as apparently unpublished in the 1981 *Collected*, but I have since traced its anonymous revised publication in *Outlook*, 31 January 1903. The story 'The Wheat' was first published posthumously in *Time and Tide*, 20, February 1954. The essay 'An Old Servant' was first published in the *New Statesman*, II, 28, 18 October 1913. The text of the play *The China Bowl* used here follows Charlotte Mew's typescript in the British Library (Additional MSS. 57755), which is very close to the BBC text (broadcast on the West of England service, 12 November 1953) printed in the 1981 *Collected*, apart from different stage directions required for radio and the substitution of 'any man' for Mew's 'the dying Christ' on page 112. (The last few lines of the play were omitted in error from the 1981 *Collected*, where the short story 'Some Ways of Love' was listed as first published in *Pall Mall Magazine*, XXIV, September 1901 instead of July.)

In the poem 'Rooms', I have removed the brackets which have hitherto always been printed round the word 'two', despite their somewhat comic effect. These brackets occur in the typescript (Additional MSS. 57755), where the whole poem is also crossed through in pencil. Mew sent out her work to a professional typist;

presumably Mew had bracketed the word 'two' while considering whether it was superfluous and forgot to remove the brackets, which the typist simply copied, so that Mew then crossed through that copy. In the subtitle of the poem 'Péri en mer', I have corrected Mew's spelling of the Breton place-name Camaret (not Cameret).

Editions

The Farmer's Bride, London: Poetry Bookshop, 1916
The Farmer's Bride (with eleven new poems), London: Poetry Bookshop, 1921 (published as *Saturday Market*, New York: Macmillan, 1921; and reissued by the Poetry Bookshop, 1929)
The Rambling Sailor, London: Poetry Bookshop, 1929
Collected Poems, London: Duckworth, 1953, with a Memoir by Alida Monro
Collected Poems and Prose, ed. Val Warner, Manchester: Carcanet, 1981; London: Virago, 1982

Further Reading

The Benedictines of Stanbrook, *In a Great Tradition, Tribute to Dame Laurentia McLachlan Abbess of Stanbrook*, London: John Murray, 1956
Blunt, Wilfrid, *Cockerell*, London: Hamish Hamilton, 1964
Boll, Theophilus E.M. 'The Mystery of Charlotte Mew and May Sinclair: An Inquiry', *Bulletin of the New York Public Library* (September 1970), LXXIV, 3, 445-53
— *Miss May Sinclair: Novelist*, Rutherford: Fairleigh Dickinson University Press, 1973
Carswell, John, *Lives and Letters (A.R. Orage; Beatrice Hastings; Katherine Mansfield; John Middleton Murry; S.S. Koteliansky)*, London: Faber, 1978
Collins, Vere H., *Talks with Thomas Hardy at Max Gate 1920-22*, London: Duckworth, 1928
Davidow, Mary C., 'Charlotte Mew: Biography and Criticism' (Brown University Ph.D. thesis), 1960
— 'The Charlotte Mew – May Sinclair Relationship: A Reply', *Bulletin of the New York Public Library* (March 1971), LXXV, 3, 295-300
Fitzgerald, Penelope, *Charlotte Mew and Her Friends*, London: Collins, 1984
Grant, Joy, *Harold Monro and the Poetry Bookshop*, London: Routledge and Kegan Paul, 1967

Greener, Amy, *A Lover of Books: The Life and Literary Papers of Lucy Harrison*, London: Dent, 1916
Greer, Germaine, *Slip-shod Sibyls*, London: Viking, 1995
Holroyd, Michael, *Unreceived Opinions*, London: Heinemann, 1973
Jeffreys, Sheila, *The Spinster and Her Enemies: Feminism and Sexuality 1880-1930*, London: Pandora, 1985
Leighton, Angela, *Victorian Women Poets: Writing against the Heart*, Hemel Hempstead: Harvester/Wheatsheaf, 1992
May, James Lewis, *John Lane and the Nineties*, London: John Lane, 1936
Meynell, Viola, ed., *Friends of a Lifetime: Letters to Sydney Carlyle Cockerell*, London: Cape, 1940
— *The Best of Friends: Further Letters to Sydney Carlyle Cockerell*, London: Rupert Hart-Davis, 1956
Mix, Katherine Lyon, *A Study in Yellow*, Lawrence and London: University of Kansas Press and Constable, 1960
Sharp, Evelyn, *Unfinished Adventure*, London: John Lane, 1933
Stock, Noel, *The Life of Ezra Pound*, Harmondsworth: Penguin, 1974
Swinnerton, Frank, *The Georgian Literary Scene 1910-1935*, London: Hutchinson, 1969
Syrett, Netta, *The Sheltering Tree*, London: Geoffrey Bles, 1939
Warner, Val, 'Mary Magdalene and the Bride: the Work of Charlotte Mew', *Poetry Nation* (1975), 4, 92-106
— 'New Light on Charlotte Mew', *PN Review* 117 (1997), 44-48
Watts, Marjorie, 'Memories of Charlotte Mew', *PEN Broadsheet* (autumn 1982), 13, 12-13
— *Mrs Sappho: The Life of C.A. Dawson Scott, Mother of International P.E.N.*, London: Duckworth, 1987

THE FARMER'S BRIDE (1916)

To ——

He asked life of Thee and Thou gavest him a long life:
even for ever and ever.

The Farmer's Bride

Three Summers since I chose a maid,
Too young maybe – but more's to do
At harvest-time than bide and woo.
        When us was wed she turned afraid
Of love and me and all things human;
Like the shut of a winter's day.
Her smile went out, and 'twasn't a woman –
        More like a little frightened fay.
                One night, in the Fall, she runned away.

'Out 'mong the sheep, her be,' they said,
'Should properly have been abed;
But sure enough she wasn't there
Lying awake with her wide brown stare.
So over seven-acre field and up-along across the down
We chased her, flying like a hare
Before our lanterns. To Church-Town
        All in a shiver and a scare
We caught her, fetched her home at last
        And turned the key upon her, fast.

She does the work about the house
As well as most, but like a mouse:
Happy enough to chat and play
With birds and rabbits and such as they,
So long as men-folk keep away.
'Not near, not near!' her eyes beseech
When one of us comes within reach.
The women say that beasts in stall
Look round like children at her call.
I've hardly heard her speak at all.

Shy as a leveret, swift as he,
Straight and slight as a young larch tree,
Sweet as the first wild violets, she,
To her wild self. But what to me?

The short days shorten and the oaks are brown,
The blue smoke rises to the low grey sky,
One leaf in the still air falls slowly down,
A magpie's spotted feathers lie
On the black earth spread white with rime,
The berries redden up to Christmas-time.
What's Christmas-time without there be
Some other in the house than we!

She sleeps up in the attic there
Alone, poor maid. 'Tis but a stair
Betwixt us. Oh! my God! the down
The soft young down of her, the brown,
The brown of her – her eyes, her hair, her hair!

Fame

Sometimes in the over-heated house, but not for long,
Smirking and speaking rather loud,
I see myself among the crowd,
Where no one fits the singer to his song,
Or sifts the unpainted from the painted faces
Of the people who are always on my stair;
They were not with me when I walked in heavenly places;
But could I spare
In the blind Earth's great silences and spaces,
The din, the scuffle, the long stare
If I went back and it was not there?
Back to the old known things that are the new,
The folded glory of the gorse, the sweet-briar air,
To the larks that cannot praise us, knowing nothing of what we do
And the divine, wise trees that do not care
Yet, to leave Fame, still with such eyes and that bright hair!
God! If I might! And before I go hence
Take in her stead
To our tossed bed,
One little dream, no matter how small, how wild.
Just now, I think I found it in a field, under a fence –
A frail, dead, new-born lamb, ghostly and pitiful and white,
A blot upon the night,
The moon's dropped child!

The Narrow Door

The narrow door, the narrow door
On the three steps of which the café children play
Mostly at shop with pebbles from the shore,
It is always shut this narrow door
But open for a little while to-day.

And round it, each with pebbles in his hand,
A silenced crowd the café children stand
To see the long box jerking down the bend
Of twisted stair; then set on end,
Quite filling up the narrow door
Till it comes out and does not go in any more.

    Along the quay you see it wind,
The slow black line. Someone pulls up the blind
Of the small window just above the narrow door –
    'Tiens! que veux-tu acheter?' Renée cries,
    'Mais, pour quat'sous, des oignons,' Jean replies
And one pays down with pebbles from the shore.

The Fête

  To-night again the moon's white mat
    Stretches across the dormitory floor
While outside, like an evil cat
  The *pion* prowls down the dark corridor,
  Planning, I know, to pounce on me, in spite
For getting leave to sleep in town last night.
But it was none of us who made that noise,
  Only the old brown owl that hoots and flies
Out of the ivy – he will say it was us boys –
  Seigneur mon Dieu! the *sacré* soul of spies!
  He would like to catch each dream that lies
    Hidden behind our sleepy eyes:
Their dream? But mine – it is the moon and the wood that sees;
All my long life how I shall hate the trees!

In the *Place d'Armes*, the dusty planes, all Summer through
Dozed with the market women in the sun and scarcely stirred
To see the quiet things that crossed the Square –,
A tiny funeral, the flying shadow of a bird,
The hump-backed barber Célestin Lemaire,
Old madame Michel in her three-wheeled chair,
And filing past to Vespers, two and two,
The *demoiselles* of the *pensionnat*.
Towed like a ship through the harbour bar,
Safe into port, where *le petit Jésus*
Perhaps makes nothing of the look they shot at you:
Si, c'est défendu, mais que voulez-vous?
It was the sun. The sunshine weaves
A pattern on dull stones: the sunshine leaves
The portraiture of dreams upon the eyes
Before it dies:
All Summer through
The dust hung white upon the drowsy planes
Till suddenly they woke with the Autumn rains.

It is not only the little boys
Who have hardly got away from toys,
But I, who am seventeen next year,
Some nights, in bed, have grown cold to hear
That lonely passion of the rain
Which makes you think of being dead,
And of somewhere living to lay your head
As if you were a child again,
Crying for one thing, known and near
Your empty heart, to still the hunger and the fear
That pelts and beats with it against the pane.

But I remember smiling too
At all the sun's soft tricks and those Autumn dreads
In winter time, when the grey light broke slowly through
The frosted window-lace to drag us shivering from our beds.
And when at dusk the singing wind swung down
Straight from the stars to the dark country roads

Beyond the twinkling town,
Striking the leafless poplar boughs as he went by,
Like some poor, stray dog by the wayside lying dead,
We left behind us the old world of dread,
I and the wind as we strode whistling on under the Winter sky.

And then in Spring for three days came the Fair
Just as the planes were starting into bud
Above the caravans: you saw the dancing bear
Pass on his chain; and heard the jingle and the thud.
Only four days ago
They let you out of this dull show
To slither down the *montagne russe* and chaff the man *à la tête de veau* –
Hit, slick, the bull's eye at the *tir,*
Spin round and round till your head went queer
On the *porcs-roulants. Oh! là là! la fête*
Va pour du vin, et le tête-a-tête
With the girl who sugars the *gaufres! Pauvrette,*
How thin she was; but she smiled, you bet,
As she took your tip – 'One does not forget
The good days, Monsieur.' Said with a grace,
But *sacrebleu!* what a ghost of a face!
And no fun too for the *demoiselles*
Of the *pensionnat*, who were hurried past,
With their *'Oh, que c'est beau – Ah, qu'elle est belle!'*
A lap-dog's life from first to last!
The good nights are not made for sleep, nor the good days for dreaming in,
And at the end in the big Circus tent we sat and shook and stewed like sin!

Some children there had got – but where?
Sent from the south, perhaps – a red bouquet
Of roses, sweetening the fetid air
With scent from gardens by some far away blue bay.
They threw one at the dancing bear;
The white clown caught it. From St. Rémy's tower
The deep, slow bell tolled out the hour;
The black clown, with his dirty grin
Lay, sprawling in the dust, as She rode in.

She stood on a white horse – and suddenly you saw the bend
   Of a far-off road at dawn, with knights riding by,
A field of spears – and then the gallant day
Go out in storm, with ragged clouds low down, sullen and grey
   Against red heavens: wild and awful, such a sky
   As witnesses against you at the end
Of a great battle; bugles blowing, blood and dust –
The old *Morte d' Arthur*, fight you must –.
   It died in anger. But it was not death
   That had you by the throat, stopping your breath.
She looked like Victory. She rode my way.

She laughed at the black clown and then she flew
      A bird above us, on the wing
Of her white arms; and you saw through
A rent in the old tent, a patch of sky
With one dim star. She flew, but not so high –
      And then she did not fly;
She stood in the bright moonlight at the door
Of a strange room, she threw her slippers on the floor –
            Again, again
      You heard the patter of the rain,
      The starving rain – it was this Thing,
Summer was this, the gold mist in your eyes; –
            Oh God! it dies,
            But after death –,
   To-night the splendour and the sting
   Blows back and catches at your breath,
The smell of beasts, the smell of dust, the scent of all the roses in the world, the sea,
      the Spring,
The beat of drums, the pad of hoofs, music, the dream, the dream, the Enchanted
      Thing!

   At first you scarcely saw her face,
   You knew the maddening feet were there,
What called was that half-hidden, white unrest
To which now and then she pressed
   Her finger tips; but as she slackened pace

And turned and looked at you it grew quite bare:
There was not anything you did not dare: –
Like trumpeters the hours passed until the last day of the Fair.

In the *Place d'Armes* all afternoon
The building birds had sung 'Soon, soon,'
The shuttered streets slept sound that night,
It was full moon:
The path into the wood was almost white,
The trees were very still and seemed to stare:
Not far before your soul the Dream flits on,
But when you touch it, it is gone
And quite alone your soul stands there.

Mother of Christ, no one has seen your eyes: how can men pray
Even unto you?
There were only wolves' eyes in the wood –
My Mother is a woman too:
Nothing is true that is not good,
With that quick smile of hers, I have heard her say; –
I wish I had gone back home to-day;
I should have watched the light that so gently dies
From our high window, in the Paris skies,
The long, straight chain
Of lamps hung out along the Seine:
I would have turned to her and let the rain
Beat on her breast as it does against the pane; –
Nothing will be the same again; –
There is something strange in my little Mother's eyes,
There is something new in the old heavenly air of Spring –
The smell of beasts, the smell of dust – *The Enchanted Thing!*

All my life long I shall see moonlight on the fern
And the black trunks of trees. Only the hair
Of any woman can belong to God.
The stalks are cruelly broken where we trod,
There had been violets there,
I shall not care
As I used to do when I see the bracken burn.

Beside the Bed

Someone has shut the shining eyes, straightened and folded
   The wandering hands quietly covering the unquiet breast:
So, smoothed and silenced you lie, like a child, not again to be questioned or scolded;
   But, for you, not one of us believes that this is rest.

Not so to close the windows down can cloud and deaden
   The blue beyond: or to screen the wavering flame subdue its breath:
Why, if I lay my cheek to your cheek, your grey lips, like dawn, would quiver and redden,
   Breaking into the old, odd smile at this fraud of death.

Because all night you have not turned to us or spoken
   It is time for you to wake; your dreams were never very deep:
I, for one, have seen the thin, bright, twisted threads of them dimmed suddenly and broken,
   This is only a most piteous pretence of sleep!

In Nunhead Cemetery

It is the clay that makes the earth stick to his spade;
      He fills in holes like this year after year;
The others have gone; they were tired, and half afraid,
      But I would rather be standing here;

There is nowhere else to go. I have seen this place
      From the windows of the train that's going past
Against the sky. This is rain on my face –
      It was raining here when I saw it last.

There is something horrible about a flower;
      This, broken in my hand, is one of those
He threw in just now: it will not live another hour;
      There are thousands more: you do not miss a rose.

One of the children hanging about
    Pointed at the whole dreadful heap and smiled
This morning, after THAT was carried out;
    There is something terrible about a child.

We were like children, last week, in the Strand;
    That was the day you laughed at me
Because I tried to make you understand
    The cheap, stale chap I used to be
    Before I saw the things you made me see.

This is not a real place; perhaps by-and-by
    I shall wake – I am getting drenched with all this rain:
To-morrow I will tell you about the eyes of the Crystal Palace train
    Looking down on us, and you will laugh and I shall see what you see again.

        Not here, not now. We said 'Not yet
        Across our low stone parapet
    Will the quick shadows of the sparrows fall.'

        But still it was a lovely thing
        Through the grey months to wait for Spring
        With the birds that go a-gypsying
    In the parks till the blue seas call.
        And next to these, you used to care
        For the lions in Trafalgar Square,
Who'll stand and speak for London when her bell of Judgment tolls –
        And the gulls at Westminster that were
        The old sea-captains' souls.
To-day again the brown tide splashes, step by step, the river stair,
        And the gulls are there!

By a month we have missed our Day:
    The children would have hung about
Round the carriage and over the way
    As you and I came out.

We should have stood on the gulls' black cliffs and heard the sea
    And seen the moon's white track,
I would have called, you would have come to me
    And kissed me back.

You have never done that: I do not know
    Why I stood staring at your bed
And heard you, though you spoke so low,
    But could not reach your hands, your little head.
There was nothing we could not do, you said,
    And you went, and I let you go!

Now I will burn you back, I will burn you through,
    Though I am damned for it we two will lie
    And burn, here where the starlings fly
    To these white stones from the wet sky – ;
    Dear, you will say this is not I –
It would not be you, it would not be you!

If for only a little while
    You will think of it you will understand,
      If you will touch my sleeve and smile
    As you did that morning in the Strand
        I can wait quietly with you
        Or go away if you want me to –
    God! What is God? but your face has gone and your hand!
        Let me stay here too.

      When I was quite a little lad
    At Christmas time we went half mad
      For joy of all the toys we had,
And then we used to sing about the sheep
      The shepherds watched by night;
We used to pray to Christ to keep
      Our small souls safe till morning light – ;
I am scared, I am staying with you to-night –
                Put me to sleep.

I shall stay here: here you can see the sky;
The houses in the streets are much too high;
    There is no one left to speak to there;
    Here they are everywhere,
And just above them fields and fields of roses lie –
If he would dig it all up again they would not die.

The Pedlar

Lend me, a little while, the key
  That locks your heavy heart, and I'll give you back –
Rarer than books and ribbons and beads bright to see,
  This little Key of Dreams out of my pack.

The road, the road, beyond men's bolted doors,
  There shall I walk and you go free of me,
For yours lies North across the moors,
  And mine South. To what sea?

How if we stopped and let our solemn selves go by,
  While my gay ghost caught and kissed yours, as ghosts don't do,
And by the wayside this forgotten you and I
  Sat, and were twenty-two?

Give me the key that locks your tired eyes,
  And I will lend you this one from my pack,
Brighter than coloured beads and painted books that make men wise:
  Take it. No, give it back!

Pécheresse

Down the long quay the slow boats glide,
  While here and there a house looms white
Against the gloom of the waterside,
  And some high window throws a light
  As they sail out into the night.

At dawn they will bring in again
  To women knitting on the quay
Who wait for him, their man of men;
  I stand with them, and watch the sea
  Which may have taken mine from me.

Just so the long days come and go.
  The nights, ma Doué! the nights are cold!
Our Lady's heart is as frozen snow,
  Since this one sin I have not told;
  And I shall die or perhaps grow old

Before he comes. The foreign ships
  Bring many a one of face and name
As strange as his, to buy your lips,
  A gold piece for a scarlet shame
  Like mine. But mine was not the same.

One night was ours, one short grey day
  Of sudden sin, unshrived, untold.
He found me, and I lost the way
  To Paradise for him. I sold
  My soul for love and not for gold.

He bought my soul, but even so,
  My face is all that he has seen,
His is the only face I know,
And in the dark church, like a screen,
  It shuts God out; it comes between;

While in some narrow foreign street
  Or loitering on the crowded quay,
Who knows what others he may meet
  To turn his eyes away from me?
  Many are fair to such as he!

There is but one for such as I
  To love, to hate, to hunger for;
I shall, perhaps, grow old and die,
  With one short day to spend and store,
  One night, in all my life, no more.

Just so the long days come and go,
  Yet this one sin I will not tell
Though Mary's heart is as frozen snow
And all nights are cold for one warmed too well.
  But, oh! ma Doué! *the nights of Hell!*

The Changeling

Toll no bell for me, dear Father, dear Mother,
    Waste no sighs;
There are my sisters, there is my little brother
  Who plays in the place called Paradise,
Your children all, your children for ever;
      But I, so wild,
Your disgrace, with the queer brown face, was never,
  Never, I know, but half your child!

In the garden at play, all day, last summer,
      Far and away I heard
The sweet 'tweet-tweet' of a strange new-comer,
  The dearest, clearest call of a bird.
It lived down there in the deep green hollow,

My own old home, and the fairies say
The word of a bird is a thing to follow,
So I was away a night and a day.

One evening, too, by the nursery fire,
We snuggled close and sat round so still,
When suddenly as the wind blew higher,
Something scratched on the window-sill.
A pinched brown face peered in – I shivered;
No one listened or seemed to see;
The arms of it waved and the wings of it quivered,
Whoo – I knew it had come for me;
Some are as bad as bad can be!
All night long they danced in the rain,
Round and round in a dripping chain,
Threw their caps at the window-pane,
Tried to make me scream and shout
And fling the bedclothes all about:
I meant to stay in bed that night,
And if only you had left a light
They would never have got me out.

Sometimes I wouldn't speak, you see,
Or answer when you spoke to me,
Because in the long, still dusks of Spring
You can hear the whole world whispering;
The shy green grasses making love,
The feathers grow on the dear, grey dove,
The tiny heart of the redstart beat,
The patter of the squirrel's feet,
The pebbles pushing in the silver streams,
The rushes talking in their dreams,
The swish-swish of the bat's black wings,
The wild-wood bluebell's sweet ting-tings,
Humming and hammering at your ear,
Everything there is to hear
In the heart of hidden things,
But not in the midst of the nursery riot,

That's why I wanted to be quiet,
Couldn't do my sums, or sing,
Or settle down to anything.
And when, for that, I was sent upstairs
I *did* kneel down to say my prayers;
But the King who sits on your high church steeple
Has nothing to do with us fairy people!

'Times I pleased you, dear Father, dear Mother,
Learned all my lessons and liked to play,
And dearly loved the little pale brother
Whom some other bird must have called away.
Why did They bring me here to make me
Not quite bad and not quite good,
Why, unless They're wicked, do They want, in spite, to take me
Back to their wet, wild wood?
Now, every night I shall see the windows shining,
The gold lamp's glow, and the fire's red gleam,
While the best of us are twining twigs and the rest of us are whining
In the hollow by the stream.
Black and chill are Their nights on the wold;
And They live so long and They feel no pain:
I shall grow up, but never grow old,
I shall always, always be very cold,
I shall never come back again!

Ken

The town is old and very steep,
A place of bells and cloisters and grey towers,
And black clad people walking in their sleep –
A nun, a priest, a woman taking flowers
To her new grave; and watched from end to end
By the great Church above, through the still hours:
But in the morning and the early dark

The children wake to dart from doors and call
Down the wide, crooked street, where, at the bend,
    Before it climbs up to the park,
Ken's is the gabled house facing the Castle wall.

When first I came upon him there
Suddenly, on the half-lit stair,
I think I hardly found a trace
Of likeness to a human face
  In his. And I said then
If in His image God made men,
Some other must have made poor Ken –
But for his eyes which looked at you
As two red, wounded stars might do.

He scarcely spoke, you scarcely heard,
    His voice broke off in little jars
To tears sometimes. An uncouth bird
  He seemed as he ploughed up the street,
Groping, with knarred, high-lifted feet
  And arms thrust out as if to beat
    Always against a threat of bars.

  And oftener than not there'd be
  A child just higher than his knee
Trotting beside him. Through his dim
  Long twilight this, at least, shone clear,
  That all the children and the deer,
    Whom every day he went to see
Out in the park, belonged to him.

    'God help the folk that next him sits
    He fidgets so, with his poor wits.'
The neighbours said on Sunday nights
When he would go to Church to 'see the lights!'
  Although for these he used to fix
  His eyes upon a crucifix
  In a dark corner, staring on

Till everybody else had gone.
And sometimes, in his evil fits,
You could not move him from his chair –
You did not look at him as he sat there,
Biting his rosary to bits.
While pointing to the Christ he tried to say
'Take it away.'

Nothing was dead:
He said 'a bird' if he picked up a broken wing,
A perished leaf or any such thing
Was just 'a rose'; and once when I had said
He must not stand and knock there any more,
He left a twig on the mat outside my door.

Not long ago
The last thrush stiffened in the snow,
While black against a sullen sky
The sighing pines stood by.
But now the wind has left our rattled pane
To flutter the hedge-sparrow's wing,
The birches in the wood are red again
And only yesterday
The larks went up a little way to sing
What lovers say
Who loiter in the lanes to-day;
The buds begin to talk of May
With learned rooks on city trees,
And if God please
With all of these
We too, shall see another Spring.

But in that red brick barn upon the hill
I wonder – can one own the deer,
And does one walk with children still
As one did here –
Do roses grow
Beneath those twenty windows in a row –

And if some night
When you have not seen any light
They cannot move you from your chair
What happens there?
I do not know.

So, when they took
Ken to that place, I did not look
After he called and turned on me
His eyes. These I shall see –

À quoi bon dire

Seventeen years ago you said
Something that sounded like Good-bye;
And everybody thinks that you are dead,
But I.

So I, as I grow stiff and cold
To this and that say Good-bye too;
And everybody sees that I am old
But you.

And one fine morning in a sunny lane
Some boy and girl will meet and kiss and swear
That nobody can love their way again
While over there
You will have smiled, I shall have tossed your hair.

The Quiet House

When we were children old Nurse used to say,
The house was like an auction or a fair
Until the lot of us were safe in bed.
It has been quiet as the country-side
Since Ted and Janey and then Mother died
And Tom crossed Father and was sent away.
After the lawsuit he could not hold up his head,
Poor Father, and he does not care
For people here, or to go anywhere.

To get away to Aunt's for that week-end
Was hard enough; (since then, a year ago,
He scarcely lets me slip out of his sight –)
At first I did not like my cousin's friend,
I did not think I should remember him:
His voice has gone, his face is growing dim
And if I like him now I do not know.
He frightened me before he smiled –
He did not ask me if he might –
He said that he would come one Sunday night,
He spoke to me as if I were a child.

No year has been like this that has just gone by;
It may be that what Father says is true,
If things are so it does not matter why:
But everything has burned, and not quite through.
The colours of the world have turned
To flame, the blue, the gold has burned
In what used to be such a leaden sky.
When you are burned quite through you die.

Red is the strangest pain to bear;
In Spring the leaves on the budding trees;
In Summer the roses are worse than these,
More terrible than they are sweet:
A rose can stab you across the street

Deeper than any knife:
And the crimson haunts you everywhere –
Thin shafts of sunlight, like the ghosts of reddened swords have struck our stair
As if, coming down, you had spilt your life.

I think that my soul is red
Like the soul of a sword or a scarlet flower:
But when these are dead
They have had their hour.

I shall have had mine, too,
For from head to feet,
I am burned and stabbed half through,
And the pain is deadly sweet.

The things that kill us seem
Blind to the death they give:
It is only in our dream
The things that kill us live.

The room is shut where Mother died,
The other rooms are as they were,
The world goes on the same outside,
The sparrows fly across the Square,
The children play as we four did there,
The trees grow green and brown and bare,
The sun shines on the dead Church spire,
And nothing lives here but the fire,
While Father watches from his chair
Day follows day
The same, or now and then, a different grey,
Till, like his hair,
Which Mother said was wavy once and bright,
They will all turn white.

To-night I heard a bell again –
Outside it was the same mist of fine rain,

The lamps just lighted down the long, dim street,
No one for me –
I think it is myself I go to meet:
I do not care; some day I *shall* not think; I shall not *be*!

On the Asylum Road

Theirs is the house whose windows – every pane –
Are made of darkly stained or clouded glass:
Sometimes you come upon them in the lane,
The saddest crowd that you will ever pass.

But still we merry town or village folk
Throw to their scattered stare a kindly grin,
And think no shame to stop and crack a joke
With the incarnate wages of man's sin.

None but ourselves in our long gallery we meet,
The moor-hen stepping from her reeds with dainty feet,
The hare-bell bowing on his stem,
Dance not with us; their pulses beat
To fainter music; nor do we to them
Make their life sweet.

The gayest crowd that they will ever pass
Are we to brother-shadows in the lane:
Our windows, too, are clouded glass
To them, yes, every pane!

Jour des Morts

(Cimetière Montparnasse)

Sweetheart, is this the last of all our posies
   And little festivals, my flowers are they
But white and wistful ghosts of gayer roses
   Shut with you in this grim garden? Not to-day,
Ah! no! come out with me before the grey gate closes
   It is your fête and here is your bouquet!

The Forest Road

The forest road,
The infinite straight road stretching away
World without end: the breathless road between the walls
Of the black listening trees: the hushed, grey road
Beyond the window that you shut to-night
Crying that you would look at it by day –
There is a shadow there that sings and calls
But not for you. Oh! hidden eyes that plead in sleep
Against the lonely dark, if I could touch the fear
And leave it kissed away on quiet lids –
If I could hush these hands that are half-awake,
Groping for me in sleep I could go free.
I wish that God would take them out of mine
And fold them like the wings of frightened birds
Shot cruelly down, but fluttering into quietness so soon,
Broken, forgotten things; there is no grief for them in the green Spring
When the new birds fly back to the old trees.
But it shall not be so with you. I will look back. I wish I knew that God would stand
Smiling and looking down on you when morning comes,
To hold you, when you wake, closer than I,
So gently though: and not with famished lips or hungry arms:
He does not hurt the frailest, dearest things
As we do in the dark. See, dear, your hair –

I must unloose this hair that sleeps and dreams
About my face, and clings like the brown weed
To drowned, delivered things, tossed by the tired sea
Back to the beaches. Oh! your hair! If you had lain
A long time dead on the rough, glistening ledge
Of some black cliff, forgotten by the tide,
The raving winds would tear, the dripping brine would rust away
Fold after fold of all the loveliness
That wraps you round, and makes you, lying here,
The passionate fragrance that the roses are.
But death would spare the glory of your head
In the long sweetness of the hair that does not die:
The spray would leap to it in every storm,
The scent of the unsilenced sea would linger on
In these dark waves, and round the silence that was you –
Only the nesting gulls would hear – but there would still be whispers in your hair;
Keep them for me; keep them for me. What *is* this singing on the road
That makes all other music like the music in a dream –
Dumb to the dancing and the marching feet; you know, in dreams, you see
Old pipers playing that you cannot hear,
And ghostly drums that only seem to beat. This seems to climb:
Is it the music of a larger place? It makes our room too small: it is like a stair,
A calling stair that climbs up to a smile you scarcely see,
Dim, but so waited for; and *you* know what a smile is, how it calls,
How if I smiled you always ran to me.
Now you must sleep forgetfully, as children do.
There is a Spirit sits by us in sleep
Nearer than those who walk with us in the bright day.
I think he has a tranquil, saving face: I think he came
Straight from the hills: he may have suffered there in time gone by,
And once, from those forsaken heights, looked down,
Lonely himself, on all the lonely sorrows of the earth.
It is his kingdom – Sleep. If I could leave you there –
If, without waking you, I could get up and reach the door – !
We used to go together. – Shut, scared eyes,
Poor, desolate, desperate hands, it is not I
Who thrust you off. No, take your hands away –
I cannot strike your lonely hands. Yes, I have struck your heart,

It did not come so near. Then lie you there
Dear and wild heart behind this quivering snow
With two red stains on it: and I will strike and tear
Mine out, and scatter it to yours. Oh! throbbing dust,
You that were life, our little wind-blown hearts!
                    The road! the road!
There is a shadow there: I see my soul,
I hear my soul, singing among the trees!

Madeleine in Church

Here, in the darkness, where this plaster saint
    Stands nearer than God stands to our distress,
And one small candle shines, but not so faint
    As the far lights of everlastingness
I'd rather kneel than over there, in open day
    Where Christ is hanging, rather pray
      To something more like my own clay,
                Not too divine;
      For, once, perhaps my little saint
      Before he got his niche and crown,
    Had one short stroll about the town;
    It brings him closer, just that taint
        And anyone can wash the paint
    Off our poor faces, his and mine!

Is that why I see Monty now? equal to any saint, poor boy, as good as gold,
But still, with just the proper trace
Of earthliness on his shining wedding face;
And then gone suddenly blank and old
The hateful day of the divorce:
Stuart got his, hands down, of course
Crowing like twenty cocks and grinning like a horse:
But Monty took it hard. All said and done I liked him best, –
He was the first, he stands out clearer than the rest.

It seems too funny all we other rips
Should have immortal souls; Monty and Redge quite damnably
Keep theirs afloat while we go down like scuttled ships. –
It's funny too, how easily we sink,
One might put up a monument, I think
To half the world and cut across it 'Lost at Sea!'
I should drown Jim, poor little sparrow, if I netted him to-night –
No, it's no use this penny light –
Or my poor saint with his tin-pot crown –
The trees of Calvary are where they were,
When we are sure that we can spare
The tallest, let us go and strike it down
And leave the other two still standing there.
I, too, would ask Him to remember me
If there were any Paradise beyond this earth that I could see.

Oh! quiet Christ who never knew
The poisonous fangs that bite us through
And make us do the things we do,
See how we suffer and fight and die,
How helpless and how low we lie,
God holds You, and You hang so high,
Though no one looking long at You,
Can think You do not suffer too,
But, up there, from your still, star-lighted tree
What can You know, what can You really see
Of this dark ditch, the soul of me!

We are what we are: when I was half a child I could not sit
Watching black shadows on green lawns and red carnations burning in the sun,
Without paying so heavily for it
That joy and pain, like any mother and her unborn child were almost one.
I could hardly bear
The dreams upon the eyes of white geraniums in the dusk,
The thick, close voice of musk,
The jessamine music on the thin night air,
Or, sometimes, my own hands about me anywhere –
The sight of my own face (for it was lovely then) even the scent of my own hair,

Oh! there was nothing, nothing that did not sweep to the high seat
Of laughing gods, and then blow down and beat
My soul into the highway dust, as hoofs do the dropped roses of the street.
I think my body was my soul,
And when we are made thus
Who shall control
Our hands, our eyes, the wandering passion of our feet,
Who shall teach us
To thrust the world out of our heart; to say, till perhaps in death,
When the race is run,
And it is forced from us with our last breath
'Thy will be done'?
If it is Your will that we should be content with the tame, bloodless things,
As pale as angels smirking by, with folded wings.
Oh! I know Virtue, and the peace it brings!
The temperate, well-worn smile
The one man gives you, when you are evermore his own:
And afterwards the child's, for a little while,
With its unknowing and all-seeing eyes
So soon to change, and make you feel how quick
The clock goes round. If one had learned the trick –
(How does one though?) quite early on,
Of long green pastures under placid skies,
One might be walking now with patient truth.
What did we ever care for it, who have asked for youth,
When, oh! my God! this is going or has gone?

There is a portrait of my mother, at nineteen,
With the black spaniel, standing by the garden seat,
The dainty head held high against the painted green
And throwing out the youngest smile, shy, but half haughty and half sweet.
Her picture then: but simply Youth, or simply Spring
To me to-day: a radiance on the wall,
So exquisite, so heart-breaking a thing
Beside the mask that I remember, shrunk and small,
Sapless and lined like a dead leaf,
All that was left of oh! the loveliest face, by time and grief!

And in the glass, last night, I saw a ghost behind my chair –
Yet why remember it, when one can still go moderately gay – ?
Or could – with any one of the old crew,
But oh! these boys! the solemn way
They take you, and the things they say –
This 'I have only as long as you'
When you remind them you are not precisely twenty-two –
Although at heart perhaps – God! if it were
Only the face, only the hair!
If Jim had written to me as he did to-day
A year ago – and now it leaves me cold –
I know what this means, old, old, *old!*
Et avec ça – mais on a vécu, tout se paie.

That is not always true: there was my Mother – (well at least the dead are free!)
Yoked to the man that Father was; yoked to the woman I am, Monty too;
The little portress at the Convent School, stewing in hell so patiently;
The poor, fair boy who shot himself at Aix. And what of me – and what of me?
But I, I paid for what I had, and they for nothing. No, one cannot see
How it shall be made up to them in some serene eternity.
If there were fifty heavens God could not give us back the child who went or never came;
Here, on our little patch of this great earth, the sun of any darkened day,
Not one of all the starry buds hung on the hawthorn trees of last year's May,
No shadow from the sloping fields of yesterday;
For every hour they slant across the hedge a different way,
The shadows are never the same.

'Find rest in Him' One knows the parsons' tags –
Back to the fold, across the evening fields, like any flock of baa-ing sheep:
Yes, it may be, when He has shorn, led us to slaughter, torn the bleating soul in us to rags,
For so He giveth His belovèd sleep.
Oh! He will take us stripped and done,
Driven into His heart. So we are won:
Then safe, safe are we? in the shelter of His everlasting wings –
I do not envy Him His victories. His arms are full of broken things.

But I shall not be in them. Let Him take
The finer ones, the easier to break.

And they are not gone, yet, for me, the lights, the colours, the perfumes,
Though now they speak rather in sumptuous rooms,
In silks and in gem-like wines;
Here, even, in this corner where my little candle shines
And overhead the lancet-window glows
With golds and crimsons you could almost drink
To know how jewels taste, just as I used to think
There was the scent in every red and yellow rose
Of all the sunsets. But this place is grey,
And much too quiet. No one here,
Why, this is awful, this is fear!
Nothing to see, no face,
Nothing to hear except your heart beating in space
As if the world was ended. Dead at last!
Dead soul, dead body, tied together fast.
These to go on with and alone, to the slow end:
No one to sit with, really, or to speak to, friend to friend:
Out of the long procession, black or white or red
Not one left now to say 'Still I am here, then see you, dear, lay here your head.'
Only the doll's house looking on the Park
To-night, all nights, I know, when the man puts the lights out, very dark.
With, upstairs, in the blue and gold box of a room, just the maids' footsteps overhead,
Then utter silence and the empty world – the room – the bed –
The corpse! No, not quite dead, while this cries out in me,
But nearly: very soon to be
A handful of forgotten dust –
There must be someone. Christ! there must,
Tell me there *will* be some one. Who?
If there were no one else, could it be You?

How old was Mary out of whom you cast
So many devils? Was she young or perhaps for years
She had sat staring, with dry eyes, at this and that man going past
Till suddenly she saw You on the steps of Simon's house
And stood and looked at You through tears.
I think she must have known by those
The thing, for what it was that had come to her.
For some of us there is a passion, I suppose

So far from earthly cares and earthly fears
That in its stillness you can hardly stir
Or in its nearness, lift your hand,
So great that you have simply got to stand
Looking at it through tears, through tears.
Then straight from these there broke the kiss,
I think You must have known by this
The thing, for what it was, that had come to You:
She did not love You like the rest,
It was in her own way, but at the worst, the best,
She gave you something altogether new.
And through it all, from her, no word,
She scarcely saw You, scarcely heard:
Surely You knew when she so touched You with her hair,
Or by the wet cheek lying there,
And while her perfume clung to You from head to feet all through the day
That You can change the things for which we care,
But even You, unless You kill us, not the way.

This, then was peace for her, but passion too.
I wonder was it like a kiss that once I knew,
The only one that I would care to take
Into the grave with me, to which if there were afterwards, to wake.
Almost as happy as the carven dead
In some dim chancel lying head by head
We slept with it, but face to face, the whole night through –
One breath, one throbbing quietness, as if the thing behind our lips was endless life,
Lost, as I woke, to hear in the strange earthly dawn, his 'Are you there?'
And lie still, listening to the wind outside, among the firs.

So Mary chose the dream of Him for what was left to her of night and day,
It is the only truth: it is the dream in us that neither life nor death nor any other thing can take away:
But if she had not touched Him in the doorway of the dream could she have cared so much?
She was a sinner, we are what we are: the spirit afterwards, but first, the touch.

And He has never shared with me my haunted house beneath the trees
Of Eden and Calvary, with its ghosts that have not any eyes for tears,
And the happier guests who would not see, or if they did, remember these,
Though they lived there a thousand years.
Outside, too gravely looking at me, He seems to stand,
And looking at Him, if my forgotten spirit came
Unwillingly back, what could it claim
Of those calm eyes, that quiet speech,
Breaking like a slow tide upon the beach,
The scarred, not quite human hand? –
Unwillingly back to the burden of old imaginings
When it has learned so long not to think, not to be,
Again, again it would speak as it has spoken to me of things
That I shall not see!

I cannot bear to look at this divinely bent and gracious head:
When I was small I never quite believed that He was dead:
And at the Convent school I used to lie awake in bed
Thinking about His hands. It did not matter what they said,
He was alive to me, so hurt, so hurt! And most of all in Holy Week
When there was no one else to see
I used to think it would not hurt me too, so terribly,
If He had ever seemed to notice me
Or, if, for once, He would only speak.

Exspecto Resurrectionem

Oh! King who hast the key
Of that dark room,
The last which prisons us but held not Thee,
Thou know'st its gloom.
Dost Thou a little love this one
Shut in to-night,
Young and so piteously alone,
Cold – out of sight?
Thou know'st how hard and bare
The pillow of that new-made narrow bed,
Then leave not there
So dear a head!

Additional poems included in* THE FARMER'S BRIDE, *1921 edition

On the Road to the Sea

We passed each other, turned and stopped for half an hour, then went our way,
I who make other women smile did not make you –
But no man can move mountains in a day.
So this hard thing is yet to do.

But first I want your life: – before I die I want to see
The world that lies behind the strangeness of your eyes,
There is nothing gay or green there for my gathering, it may be,
Yet on brown fields there lies
A haunting purple bloom: is there not something in grey skies
And in grey sea?
I want what world there is behind your eyes,
I want your life and you will not give it me.

Now, if I look, I see you walking down the years,
Young, and through August fields – a face, a thought, a swinging dream perched on
a stile – ;
I would have liked (so vile we are!) to have taught you tears
But most to have made you smile.

To-day is not enough or yesterday: God sees it all –
Your length on sunny lawns, the wakeful rainy nights – ; tell me – ; (how vain to ask),
but it is not a question – just a call – ;
Show me then, only your notched inches climbing up the garden wall,
I like you best when you were small.

Is this a stupid thing to say
Not having spent with you one day?
No matter; I shall never touch your hair
Or hear the little tick behind your breast,
Still it is there,
And as a flying bird
Brushes the branches where it may not rest
I have brushed your hand and heard
The child in you: I like that best

So small, so dark, so sweet; and were you also then too grave and wise?
Always I think. Then put your far off little hand in mine; – Oh! let it rest;
I will not stare into the early world beyond the opening eyes,
Or vex or scare what I love best.
But I want your life before mine bleeds away –
Here – not in heavenly hereafters – soon, –
I want your smile this very afternoon,
(The last of all my vices, pleasant people used to say,
I wanted and I sometimes got – the Moon!)

You know, at dusk, the last bird's cry,
And round the house the flap of the bat's low flight,
Trees that go black against the sky
And then – how soon the night!

No shadow of you on any bright road again,
And at the darkening end of this – what voice? whose kiss? As if you'd say!
It is not I who have walked with you, it will not be I who take away
Peace, peace, my little handful of the gleaner's grain
From your reaped fields at the shut of day.

Peace! Would you not rather die
Reeling, – with all the cannons at your ear?
So, at least, would I,
And I may not be here
To-night, to-morrow morning or next year.
Still I will let you keep your life a little while,
See dear?
I have made you smile.

The Sunlit House

White through the gate it gleamed and slept
In shuttered sunshine: the parched garden flowers
Their fallen petals from the beds unswept,
Like children unloved and ill-kept
Dreamed through the hours.
Two blue hydrangeas by the blistered door, burned brown,
Watched there and no one in the town
Cared to go past it night or day,
Though why this was they wouldn't say.
But, I the stranger, knew that I must stay,
Pace up the weed-grown paths and down,
Till one afternoon – there is just a doubt –
But I fancy I heard a tiny shout –
From an upper window a bird flew out –
And I went my way.

The Shade-Catchers

I think they were about as high
    As haycocks are. They went running by
Catching bits of shade in the sunny street:
'I've got one,' cried sister to brother.
    'I've got two.' 'Now I've got another.'
But scudding away on their little bare feet,
They left the shade in the sunny street.

Le Sacré-Coeur

(MONTMARTRE)

It is dark up here on the heights,
    Between the dome and the stars it is quiet too,
While down there under the crowded lights
    Flares the importunate face of you,
Dear Paris of the hot white hands, the scarlet lips, the scented hair,
        Une jolie fille à vendre, très cher;
        A thing of gaiety, a thing of sorrow,
        Bought to-night, possessed, and tossed
        Back to the mart again to-morrow,
            Worth and over, what you cost;
While half your charm is that you are
Withal, like some unpurchasable star,
    So old, so young and infinite and lost.

It is dark on the dome-capped hill,
    Serenely dark, divinely still,
Yet here is the Man who bought you first
    Dying of his immortal smart,
Your Lover, the King with the broken heart,
    Who while you, feasting, drink your fill,
            Pass round the cup
            Not looking up,
Calls down to you, 'I thirst.'

'A king with a broken heart! *Mon Dieu!*
One breaks so many, *cela peut se croire,*
To remember all *c'est la mer à boire,*
And the first, *mais comme c'est vieux.*
Perhaps there is still some keepsake – or
One has possibly sold it for a song:
On ne peut pas toujours pleurer les morts,
And this One – He has been dead so long!'

Song

Love, Love to-day, my dear,
Love is not always here;
Wise maids know how soon grows sere
The greenest leaf of Spring;
But no man knoweth
Whither it goeth
When the wind bloweth
So frail a thing.

Love, Love, my dear, to-day,
If the ship's in the bay,
If the bird has come your way
That sings on summer trees;
When his song faileth
And the ship saileth
No voice availeth
To call back these.

Saturday Market

Bury your heart in some deep green hollow
    Or hide it up in a kind old tree
Better still, give it the swallow
    When she goes over the sea.

In Saturday Market there's eggs a 'plenty
    And dead-alive ducks with their legs tied down,
Grey old gaffers and boys of twenty –
    Girls and the women of the town –
Pitchers and sugar-sticks, ribbons and laces,
    Posies and whips and dicky-birds' seed,
Silver pieces and smiling faces,
    In Saturday Market they've all they need.

What were you showing in Saturday Market
    That set it grinning from end to end
Girls and gaffers and boys of twenty – ?
    Cover it close with your shawl, my friend –
Hasten you home with the laugh behind you,
    Over the down –, out of sight,
Fasten your door, though no one will find you
    No one will look on a Market night.

See, you, the shawl is wet, take out from under
    The red dead thing –. In the white of the moon
On the flags does it stir again? Well, and no wonder!
    Best make an end of it; bury it soon.
If there is blood on the hearth who'll know it?
    Or blood on the stairs,
When a murder is over and done why show it?
    In Saturday Market nobody cares.

Then lie you straight on your bed for a short, short weeping
    And still, for a long, long rest,
There's never a one in the town so sure of sleeping
    As you, in the house on the down with a hole in your breast.

Think no more of the swallow,
Forget, you, the sea,
Never again remember the deep green hollow
Or the top of the kind old tree!

Arracombe Wood

Some said, because he wud'n spaik
Any words to women but Yes and No,
Nor put out his hand for Parson to shake
He mun be bird-witted. But I do go
By the lie of the barley that he did sow,
And I wish no better thing than to hold a rake
Like Dave, in his time, or to see him mow.

Put up in churchyard a month ago,
'A bitter old soul,' they said, but it wadn't so.
His heart were in Arracombe Wood where he'd used to go
To sit and talk wi' his shadder till sun went low,
Though what it was all about us'll never know.
And there baint no mem'ry in the place
Of th' old man's footmark, nor his face;
Arracombe Wood do think more of a crow –
'Will be violets there in the Spring: in Summer time the spider's lace;
And come the Fall, the whizzle and race
Of the dry, dead leaves when the wind gies chase;
And on the Eve of Christmas, fallin' snow.

Sea Love

Tide be runnin' the great world over:
  T'was only last June month I mind that we
Was thinkin' the toss and the call in the breast of the lover
  So everlastin' as the sea.

Heer's the same little fishes that sputter and swim,
  Wi' the moon's old glim on the grey, wet sand;
An' him no more to me nor me to him
  Than the wind goin' over my hand.

The Road to Kérity

Do you remember the two old people we passed on the road to Kérity,
Resting their sack on the stones, by the drenched wayside,
Looking at us with their lightless eyes through the driving rain, and then out again
To the rocks, and the long white line of the tide:
Frozen ghosts that were children once, husband and wife, father, and mother,
Looking at us with those frozen eyes; have you ever seen anything quite so chilled or so old?
                    But we – with our arms about each other,
                        We did not feel the cold!

I Have Been Through the Gates

His heart, to me, was a place of palaces and pinnacles and shining towers;
I saw it then as we see things in dreams, – I do not remember how long I slept;
I remember the trees, and the high, white walls, and how the sun was always on the towers;
The walls are standing to-day, and the gates: I have been through the gates, I have groped, I
have crept
Back, back. There is dust in the streets, and blood; they are empty; darkness is over them;
His heart is a place with the lights gone out, forsaken by great winds and the heavenly rain,
unclean and unswept,
Like the heart of the holy city, old, blind, beautiful Jerusalem,
Over which Christ wept.

The Cenotaph

Not yet will those measureless fields be green again
Where only yesterday the wild, sweet, blood of wonderful youth was shed;
There is a grave whose earth must hold too long, too deep a stain,
Though for ever over it we may speak as proudly as we may tread.
But here, where the watchers by lonely hearths from the thrust of an inward sword have
more slowly bled,
We shall build the Cenotaph: Victory, winged, with Peace, winged too, at the column's head.
And over the stairway, at the foot – oh! here, leave desolate, passionate hands to spread
Violets, roses, and laurel, with the small, sweet, twinkling country things
Speaking so wistfully of other Springs,
From the little gardens of little places where son or sweetheart was born and bred.
In splendid sleep, with a thousand brothers
To lovers, to mothers
Here, too, lies he:
Under the purple, the green, the red,
It is all young life: it must break some women's hearts to see
Such a brave, gay coverlet to such a bed!
Only, when all is done and said,
God is not mocked and neither are the dead.

For this will stand in our Market-place –
                    Who'll sell, who'll buy
                    (Will you or I
Lie each to each with the better grace)?
While looking into every busy whore's and huckster's face
As they drive their bargains, is the Face
Of God: and some young, piteous, murdered face.

THE RAMBLING SAILOR (1929)

In the Fields

Lord, when I look at lovely things which pass,
   Under old trees the shadows of young leaves
Dancing to please the wind along the grass,
   Or the gold stillness of the August sun on the August sheaves;
Can I believe there is a heavenlier world than this?
   And if there is
Will the strange heart of any everlasting thing
   Bring me these dreams that take my breath away?
They come at evening with the home-flying rooks and the scent of hay,
   Over the fields. They come in Spring.

From a Window

Up here, with June, the sycamore throws
   Across the window a whispering screen;
I shall miss the sycamore more, I suppose,
Than anything else on this earth that is out in green.
But I mean to go through the door without fear,
Not caring much what happens here
   When I'm away: –
How green the screen is across the panes
Or who goes laughing along the lanes
With my old lover all the summer day.

Not for that City

Not for that city of the level sun,
      Its golden streets and glittering gates ablaze –
      The shadeless, sleepless city of white days,
White nights, or nights and days that are as one –
We weary, when all is said, all thought, all done.
      We strain our eyes beyond this dusk to see
      What, from the threshold of eternity
We shall step into. No, I think we shun
The splendour of that everlasting glare,
   The clamour of that never-ending song.
   And if for anything we greatly long,
It is for some remote and quiet stair
      Which winds to silence and a space of sleep
      Too sound for waking and for dreams too deep.

Rooms

I remember rooms that have had their part
   In the steady slowing down of the heart.
The room in Paris, the room at Geneva,
The little damp room with the seaweed smell,
And that ceaseless maddening sound of the tide –
   Rooms where for good or for ill – things died.
But there is the room where we two lie dead,
Though every morning we seem to wake and might just as well seem to sleep again
   As we shall somewhere in the other quieter, dustier bed
   Out there in the sun – in the rain.

Monsieur qui passe
(Quai Voltaire)

A purple blot against the dead white door
In my friend's rooms, bathed in their vile pink light,
I had not noticed her before
She snatched my eyes and threw them back at me:
She did not speak till we came out into the night,
Paused at this bench beside the kiosk on the quay.

God knows precisely what she said –
I left to her the twisted skein,
Though here and there I caught a thread, –
Something, at first, about 'the lamps along the Seine,
And Paris, with that witching card of Spring
Kept up her sleeve, – why you could see
The trick done on these freezing winter nights!
While half the kisses of the Quay –
Youth, hope, – the whole enchanted string
Of dreams hung on the Seine's long line of lights.'

Then suddenly she stripped, the very skin
Came off her soul, – a mere girl clings
Longer to some last rag, however thin,
When she has shown you – well – all sorts of things:
'If it were daylight – oh! one keeps one's head –
But fourteen years! – No one has ever guessed –
The whole thing starts when one gets to bed –
Death? – If the dead would tell us they had rest!
But your eyes held it as I stood there by the door –
One speaks to Christ – one tries to catch His garment's hem –
One hardly says as much to Him – no more:
It was not you, it was your eyes – I spoke to them.'

She stopped like a shot bird that flutters still,
And drops, and tries to run again, and swerves.
The tale should end in some walled house upon a hill.
My eyes, at least, won't play such havoc there, –

Or hers – But she had hair! – blood dipped in gold;
And here she left me throwing back the first odd stare.
Some sort of beauty once, but turning yellow, getting old.
Pouah! These women and their nerves!
God! but the night *is* cold!

Do Dreams Lie Deeper?

His dust looks up to the changing sky
Through daisies' eyes;
And when a swallow flies
Only so high
He hears her going by
As daisies do. He does not die
In this brown earth where he was glad enough to lie.

But looking up from that other bed,
'There is something more my own,' he said,
'Than hands or feet or this restless head
That must be buried when I am dead.
The Trumpet may wake every other sleeper.
Do dreams lie deeper – ?
And what sunrise
When these are shut shall open their little eyes?
They are my children, they have very lovely faces –
And how does one bury the breathless dreams?
They are not of the earth and not of the sea,
They have no friends here but the flakes of the falling snow;
You and I will go down two paces –
Where do they go?'

Domus Caedet Arborem

Ever since the great planes were murdered at the end of the gardens
    The city, to me, at night has the look of a Spirit brooding crime;
As if the dark houses watching the trees from dark windows
        Were simply biding their time.

Fin de fête

Sweetheart, for such a day
    One mustn't grudge the score;
Here, then, it's all to pay,
    It's Good-night at the door.

Good-night and good dreams to you, –
    Do you remember the picture-book thieves
Who left two children sleeping in a wood the long night through,
    And how the birds came down and covered them with leaves?

So you and I should have slept, – But now,
    Oh, what a lonely head!
With just the shadow of a waving bough
    In the moonlight over your bed.

Again

One day, not here, you will find a hand
    Stretched out to you as you walk down some heavenly street;
You will see a stranger scarred from head to feet;
But when he speaks to you you will not understand,
Nor yet who wounded him nor why his wounds are sweet.
    And saying nothing, letting go his hand,
    You will leave him in the heavenly street –
        So we shall meet!

Epitaph

He loved gay things
Yet with the brave
He laughed when he was covered with grey wings,
– Asking the darkest angel for bright things
And the angel gave –
So with a smile he overstepped the grave.

Friend, Wherefore – ?

I will not count the years – there are days too –
And to-night again I have said
'What if you should be lying dead?'
Well, if it were so, I could only lay my head
Quietly on the pillow of my bed
Thinking of Him on whom poor sufferers cried
Suffering Himself so much before He died:
And then of Judas walking three years by His side –
How Judas kissed Him – how He was crucified.
Always when I see you
I see those two;
Oh! God it is true
We do not, all of us, know what we do;
But Judas knew.

I so liked Spring

I so liked Spring last year
Because you were here; –
The thrushes too –
Because it was these you so liked to hear –
I so liked you.

This year's a different thing, –
I'll not think of you.
But I'll like Spring because it is simply Spring
As the thrushes do.

Here lies a Prisoner

Leave him: he's quiet enough: and what matter
Out of his body or in, you can scatter
The frozen breath of his silenced soul, of his outraged soul to the winds that rave:
Quieter now than he used to be, but listening still to the magpie chatter
Over his grave.

May, 1915

Let us remember Spring will come again
To the scorched, blackened woods, where the wounded trees
Wait, with their old wise patience for the heavenly rain,
Sure of the sky: sure of the sea to send its healing breeze,
Sure of the sun. And even as to these
Surely the Spring, when God shall please,
Will come again like a divine surprise
To those who sit to-day with their great Dead, hands in their hands, eyes in their eyes,
At one with Love, at one with Grief: blind to the scattered things and changing skies.

June, 1915

Who thinks of June's first rose to-day?
Only some child, perhaps, with shining eyes and rough bright hair will reach it down
In a green sunny lane, to us almost as far away
As are the fearless stars from these veiled lamps of town.
What's little June to a great broken world with eyes gone dim
From too much looking on the face of grief, the face of dread?
Or what's the broken world to June and him
Of the small eager hand, the shining eyes, the rough bright head?

Ne me tangito

'This man . . . would have known who and what manner of woman this is: for she is a sinner.' – *S. Luke* vii. 39.

Odd, *You* should fear the touch,
The first that I was ever ready to let go,
I, that have not cared much
For any toy I could not break and throw
To the four winds when I had done with it. You need not fear the touch,
Blindest of all the things that I have cared for very much
In the whole gay, unbearable, amazing show.

True – for a moment – no, dull heart, you were too small,
Thinking to hide the ugly doubt behind that hurried puzzled little smile:
Only the shade, was it, you saw? but still the shade of something vile:
Oddest of all!
So I will tell you this. Last night, in sleep,
Walking through April fields I heard the far-off bleat of sheep
And from the trees about the farm, not very high,
A flight of pigeons fluttered up into an early evening mackerel sky.
Someone stood by and it was you:
About us both a great wind blew.
My breast was bared

But sheltered by my hair
I found you, suddenly, lying there,
Tugging with tiny fingers at my heart, no more afraid:
The weakest thing, the most divine
That ever yet was mine,
Something that I had strangely made,
So then it seemed –
The child for which I had not looked or ever cared,
Of whom, before, I had never dreamed.

Old Shepherd's Prayer

Up to the bed by the window, where I be lyin',
Comes bells and bleat of the flock wi' they two children's clack.
Over, from under the eaves there's the starlings flyin',
And down in yard, fit to burst his chain, yapping out at Sue I do hear young Mac.

Turning around like a falled-over sack
I can see team ploughin' in Whithy-bush field and meal carts startin' up road to Church-Town;
Saturday arternoon the men goin' back
And the women from market, trapin' home over the down.

Heavenly Master, I wud like to wake to they same green places
Where I be know'd for breakin' dogs and follerin' sheep.
And if I may not walk in th' old ways and look on th' old faces
I wud sooner sleep.

My Heart is Lame

My heart is lame with running after yours so fast
Such a long way,
Shall we walk slowly home, looking at all the things we passed
Perhaps to-day?

Home down the quiet evening roads under the quiet skies,
Not saying much,
You for a moment giving me your eyes
When you could bear my touch.

But not to-morrow. This has taken all my breath;
Then, though you look the same,
There may be something lovelier in Love's face in death
As your heart sees it, running back the way we came;
My heart is lame.

On Youth Struck Down

(FROM AN UNFINISHED ELEGY)

Oh! Death what have you to say?
'Like a bride – like a bride-groom they ride away:
You shall go back to make up the fire,
To learn patience – to learn grief,
To learn sleep when the light has quite gone out of your earthly skies,
But they have the light in their eyes
To the end of their day.'

The Trees are Down

– and he cried with a loud voice:
Hurt not the earth, neither the sea, nor the trees –
(REVELATION.)

They are cutting down the great plane-trees at the end of the gardens.
For days there has been the grate of the saw, the swish of the branches as they fall,
The crash of trunks, the rustle of trodden leaves,
With the 'Whoops' and the 'Whoas,' the loud common talk, the loud common laughs of the men, above it all.

I remember one evening of a long past Spring
Turning in at a gate, getting out of a cart, and finding a large dead rat in the mud of the drive.
I remember thinking: alive or dead, a rat was a god-forsaken thing,
But at least, in May, that even a rat should be alive.

The week's work here is as good as done. There is just one bough
On the roped bole, in the fine grey rain,
Green and high
And lonely against the sky.
(Down now! –)
And but for that,
If an old dead rat
Did once, for a moment, unmake the Spring, I might never have thought of him again.

It is not for a moment the Spring is unmade to-day;
These were great trees, it was in them from root to stem:
When the men with the 'Whoops' and the 'Whoas' have carted the whole of the whispering loveliness away
Half the Spring, for me, will have gone with them.

It is going now, and my heart has been struck with the hearts of the planes;
Half my life it has beat with these, in the sun, in the rains,
In the March wind, the May breeze,
In the great gales that came over to them across the roofs from the great seas.
There was only a quiet rain when they were dying;

They must have heard the sparrows flying,
And the small creeping creatures in the earth where they were lying –
But I, all day, I heard an angel crying:
'Hurt not the trees.'

Smile, Death

Smile, Death, see I smile as I come to you
Straight from the road and the moor that I leave behind,
Nothing on earth to me was like this wind-blown space,
Nothing was like the road, but at the end there was a vision or a face
And the eyes were not always kind.

Smile, Death, as you fasten the blades to my feet for me,
On, on let us skate past the sleeping willows dusted with snow;
Fast, fast down the frozen stream, wih the moor and the road and the vision behind,
(Show me your face, why the eyes are kind!)
And we will not speak of life or believe in it or remember it as we go.

The Rambling Sailor

In the old back streets o' Pimlico,
On the docks at Monte Video,
At the Ring o' Bells on Plymouth Hoe
He'm arter me now wheerever I go.
An' dirty nights when the wind do blow
I can hear him sing-songin' up from sea:
Oh! no man nor woman's bin friend to me
An' to-day I'm feared wheer to-morrow I'll be,
Sin' the night the moon lay whist and white
On the road goin' down to the Lizard Light
When I heard him hummin' behind me.

'Oh! look, boy, look in your sweetheart's eyes
So deep as sea an' so blue as skies;
An' 'tis better to kiss than to chide her.
If they tell 'ee no tales, they'll tell 'ee no lies
Of the little brown mouse
That creeps into the house
To lie sleepin' so quiet beside her.

'Oh! hold 'ee long, but hold 'ee light
Your true man's hand when you find him,
He'll help 'ee home on a darksome night
Wi' a somethin' bright
That he'm holdin' tight
In the hand that he keeps behind him.

'Oh! sit 'ee down to your whack o' pies,
So hot's the stew and the brew likewise,
But whiles you'm scrapin' the plates and dishes,
A'gapin' down in the shiversome sea
For the delicate mossels inside o' we
Theer's a passel o' hungry fishes.'

At the *Halte des Marins* at *Saint Nazaire*
I cussed him, sittin' astride his chair;
An' Christmas Eve on the Mary Clare
I pitched him a'down the hatch-way stair.
But 'Shoutin' and cloutin's nothing to me,
Nor the hop nor the skip nor the jump,' says he,
'For I be walkin' on every quay –'

'So look, boy, look in the dear maid's eyes
And take the true man's hand
And eat your fill o' your whack o' pies
Till you'm starin' up wheer the sea-crow flies
Wi' your head lyin' soft in the sand.'

The Call

From our low seat beside the fire
Where we have dozed and dreamed and watched the glow
Or raked the ashes, stopping so
We scarcely saw the sun or rain
Above, or looked much higher
Than this same quiet red or burned-out fire.
To-night we heard a call,
A rattle on the window-pane,
A voice on the sharp air,
And felt a breath stirring our hair,
A flame within us: Something swift and tall
Swept in and out and that was all.
Was it a bright or a dark angel? Who can know?
It left no mark upon the snow,
But suddenly it snapped the chain
Unbarred, flung wide the door
Which will not shut again;
And so we cannot sit here any more.
We must arise and go:
The world is cold without
And dark and hedged about
With mystery and enmity and doubt,
But we must go
Though yet we do not know
Who called, or what marks we shall leave upon the snow.

Absence

Sometimes I know the way
You walk, up over the bay;
It is a wind from that far sea
That blows the fragrance of your hair to me.

Or in this garden when the breeze
    Touches my trees
To stir their dreaming shadows on the grass
    I see you pass.

In sheltered beds, the heart of every rose
    Serenely sleeps to-night. As shut as those
Your guarded heart; as safe as they from the beat, beat
Of hooves that tread dropped roses in the street.

        Turn never again
        On these eyes blind with a wild rain
    Your eyes; they were stars to me. –
        There are things stars may not see.

But call, call, and though Christ stands
    Still with scarred hands
Over my mouth, I must answer. So,
I will come – He shall let me go!

To a Child in Death

You would have scoffed if we had told you yesterday
    Love made us feel, or so it was with me, like some great bird
        Trying to hold and shelter you in its strong wing; –
A gay little shadowy smile would have tossed us back such a solemn word,
        And it was not for that you were listening
        When so quietly you slipped away
With half the music of the world unheard.
What shall we do with this strange summer, meant for you, –
        Dear, if we see the winter through
        What shall be done with spring?
This, this is the victory of the Grave; here is death's sting,
That it is not strong enough, our strongest wing.

But what of His who like a Father pitieth?
His Son was also, once, a little thing,
The wistfullest child that ever drew breath,
Chased by a sword from Bethlehem and in the busy house at Nazareth
Playing with little rows of nails, watching the carpenter's hammer swing,
Long years before His hands and feet were tied
And by a hammer and the three great nails He died,
Of youth, of Spring,
Of sorrow, of loneliness, of victory the King,
Under the shadow of that wing.

Moorland Night

My face is against the grass – the moorland grass is wet –
My eyes are shut against the grass, against my lips there are the little blades,
Over my head the curlews call,
And now there is the night wind in my hair;
My heart is against the grass and the sweet earth; – it has gone still, at last.
It does not want to beat any more,
And why should it beat?
This is the end of the journey;
The Thing is found.

This is the end of all the roads –
Over the grass there is the night-dew
And the wind that drives up from the sea along the moorland road;
I hear a curlew start out from the heath
And fly off, calling through the dusk,
The wild, long, rippling call.
The Thing is found and I am quiet with the earth.
Perhaps the earth will hold it, or the wind, or that bird's cry,
But it is not for long in any life I know. This cannot stay,
Not now, not yet, not in a dying world, with me, for very long.
I leave it here:
And one day the wet grass may give it back –

One day the quiet earth may give it back –
The calling birds may give it back as they go by –
To someone walking on the moor who starves for love and will not know
Who gave it to all these to give away;
Or, if I come and ask for it again,
Oh! then, to me.

Early poems printed at the end of The Rambling Sailor

At the Convent Gate

'Why do you shrink away, and start and stare?
Life frowns to see you leaning at death's gate –
Not back, but on. Ah! sweet, it is too late:
You cannot cast these kisses from your hair.
Will God's cold breath blow kindly anywhere
Upon such burning gold? Oh! lips worn white
With waiting! Love will blossom in a night
And you shall wake to find the roses there!'

'Oh hush! He seems to stir, He lifts His Head.
He smiles. Look where He hangs against the sky.
He never smiled nor stirred, that God of pain
With tired eyes and limbs above my bed –
But loose me, this is death, I will not die –
Not while He smiles. Oh! Christ, Thine own again!'

Requiescat

Your birds that call from tree to tree
  Just overhead, and whirl and dart,
Your breeze fresh-blowing from the sea,
  And your sea singing on, Sweetheart.

Your salt scent on the thin sharp air
  Of this grey dawn's first drowsy hours,
While on the grass shines everywhere
  The yellow starlight of your flowers.

At the road's end your strip of blue
  Beyond that line of naked trees –
Strange that we should remember you
  As if you would remember these!

As if your spirit, swaying yet
  To the old passions, were not free
Of Spring's wild magic, and the fret
  Of the wilder wooing of the sea!

What threat of old imaginings,
  Half-haunted joy, enchanted pain,
Or dread of unfamiliar things
  Should ever trouble you again?

Yet you would wake and want, you said,
  The little whirr of wings, the clear
Gay notes, the wind, the golden bed
  Of the daffodil: and they are here!

Just overhead, they whirl and dart
  Your birds that call from tree to tree,
Your sea is singing on – Sweetheart,
  Your breeze is blowing from the sea.

Beyond the line of naked trees
   At the road's end, your stretch of blue –
Strange if you should remember these
   As we, ah! God! remember you!

The Little Portress

(St. Gilda de Rhuys)

The stillness of the sunshine lies
   Upon her spirit: silence seems
   To look out from its place of dreams
When suddenly she lifts her eyes
   To waken, for a little space,
   The smile asleep upon her face.

A thousand years of sun and shower,
   The melting of unnumbered snows
   Go to the making of the rose
Which blushes out its little hour.
   So old is Beauty: in its heart
   The ages seem to meet and part.

Like Beauty's self, she holds a clear
   Deep memory of hidden things –
   The music of forgotten springs –
So far she travels back, so near
   She seems to stand to patient truth
   As old as Age, as young as Youth.

That is her window, by the gate.
   Now and again her figure flits
   Across the wall. Long hours she sits
Within: on all who come to wait.
   Her Saviour too is hanging there
   A foot or so above her chair.

'Sœur Marie de l'enfant Jésus,'
You wrote it in my little book –
Your shadow-name. Your shadow-look
Is dimmer and diviner too,
But not to keep: it slips so far
Beyond us to that golden bar

Where angels, watching from their stair,
Half-envy you your tranquil days
Of prayer as exquisite as praise, –
Grey twilights softer than their glare
Of glory: all sweet human things
Which vanish with the whirr of wings.

Yet will you, when you wing your way
To whiter worlds, more whitely shine
Or shed a radiance more divine
Than here you shed from day to day –
High in His heaven a quiet star,
Be nearer God than now you are?

Afternoon Tea

Please you, excuse me, good five-o'clock people,
I've lost my last hatful of words,
And my heart's in the wood up above the church steeple,
I'd rather have tea with the birds.

Gay Kate's stolen kisses, poor Barnaby's scars,
John's losses and Mary's gains,
Oh! what do they matter, my dears, to the stars
Or the glow-worms in the lanes!

I'd rather lie under the tall elm-trees,
With old rooks talking loud overhead,
To watch a red squirrel run over my knees,
Very still on my brackeny bed.

And wonder what feathers the wrens will be taking
For lining their nests next Spring;
Or why the tossed shadow of boughs in a great wind shaking
Is such a lovely thing.

She was a Sinner

Love was my flower, and before He came –
'Master, there was a garden where it grew
Rank, with the colour of a crimson flame,
Thy flower too, but knowing not its name
Nor yet that it was Thine, I did not spare
But tore and trampled it and stained my hair,
My hands, my lips, with the red petals; see,
Drenched with the blood of Thy poor murdered flower
I stood, when suddenly the hour
Struck for me,
And straight I came and wound about Thy Feet
The strands of shame
Twined with those broken buds: till lo, more sweet,
More red, yet still the same,
Bright burning blossoms sprang around Thy brow
Beneath the thorns (I saw, I know not how,
The crown which Thou wast afterward to wear
On that immortal Tree)
And I went out and found my garden very bare,
But swept and watered it, then followed Thee.

There was another garden where to seek
Thee, first, I came in those grey hours
Of the Great Dawn, and knew Thee not till Thou didst speak
My name, that "Mary" like a flash of light
Shot from Thy lips. Thou wast "the gardener" too,
                And then I knew
That evermore our flowers,
Thine, Lord, and mine, shall be a burning white.'

Song

Oh! Sorrow, Sorrow, scarce I knew.
  Your name when, shaking down the may
In sport, a little child, I grew
  Afraid to find you at my play.
I heard it ere I looked at you;
  You sang it softly as you came
Bringing your little boughs of yew
  To fling across my gayest game.

Oh! Sorrow, Sorrow, was I fair
  That when I decked me for a bride,
You met me stepping down the stair
  And led me from my lover's side?
Was I so dear you could not spare
  The maid to love, the child to play,
But coming always unaware,
  Must bid and beckon me away?

Oh! Sorrow, Sorrow, is my bed
  So wide and warm that you must lie
Upon it; toss your weary head
  And stir my slumber with your sigh?
I left my love at your behest,
  I waved your little boughs of yew,
But, Sorrow, Sorrow, let me rest,
  For oh! I cannot sleep with you!

An Ending

You know that road beside the sea,
  Walled by the wavin' wheat,
Which winds down to the little town,
  Wind-blown and grey and up the crooked street?
      We'd used to meet
Just at the top, and when the grass was trodden down
      'Twas by our feet.
      We'd used to stand
And watch the clouds like a great fleet
  Sail over the sea and over land,
      And the gulls dart
Above our heads: and by the gate
  At the road's end, when et was late
And all the ships was showing lights on quiet nights,
      We'd used to part.

So, Sir, you think I've missed my way,
  There's nothing but the Judgment Seat –
But ef I pray perhaps I may – what's that you say –
      A golden street?
  Give me the yellow wheat!
  Et edn't *there* we'm goin' to meet!
No, I'm not mazed, I make no doubt
  That ef we don't my soul goes out
'Most like a candle in the everlasting dark.
  And what's the odds? 'Twas just a spark
      Alight for her.
      I tell you, Sir,
That God He made et brave and plain,
  Sin' He knows better than yon Book
      What's in a look
You'd go to Hell to get again.

Another hour? An hour to wait – !
  I sim I'll meet her at the gate –
You know that road beside the sea –
  The crooked street – the wavin' wheat – ?
(What's that? A lamp! Et made me start –)
  That's where our feet – we'd used to meet – on quiet nights –
My God! the ships es showing lights! –
          We'd used – to part.

A Question

If Christ was crucified – Ah! God, are we
  Not scourged, tormented, mocked and called to pay
  The sin of ages in our little day –
Has man no crown of thorns, no Calvary,
Though Christ has tasted of his agony?
  We knew no Eden and the poisoned fruit
  We did not pluck, yet from the bitter root
We sprang, maimed branches of iniquity.

Have we who share the heritage accurst
  Wrought nothing? Tainted to the end of time,
The last frail souls still suffer for the first
  Blind victims of an everlasting crime.
Ask of the Crucified, Who hangs enthroned,
If man – oh! God, man too has not atoned!

Left Behind

Wilt thou have pity? intercede for me.
So near, at last thou standest to the throne,
Thou mayest call for mercy on thine own,
As here thine own for mercy calls on thee.
Fling then my soul, thy soul, upon its knee;
Bestir these lips of mine for me to pray;
Release this spirit from its tortured clay,
Remembering that thine, its mate, is free.

I wait thy summons on a swaying floor,
Within a room half darkness and half glare.
I cannot stir – I cannot find the stair –
Thrust hands upon my heart ; it clogs my feet,
As drop by drop it drains. I stand and beat –
I stand and beat my heart against the door.

A Farewell

Remember me and smile, as smiling too,
I have remembered things that went their way –
The dolls with which I grew too wise to play –
Or over-wise – and kissed, as children do,
And so dismissed them; yes, even as you
Have done with this poor piece of painted clay –
Not wantonly, but wisely, shall we say?
As one who, haply, tunes his heart anew.

Only I wish her eyes may not be blue,
The eyes of the new angel. Ah! she may
Miss something that I found, – perhaps the clue
To those long silences of yours, which grew
Into one word. And should she not be gay,
Poor lady! Well, she too must have her day!

'There shall be no night there'

IN THE FIELDS

Across these wind-blown meadows I can see
  The far off glimmer of the little town,
  And feel the darkness slowly shutting down
To lock from day's long glare my soul and me.
  Then through my blood the coming mystery
Of night steals to my heart and turns my feet
Toward that chamber in the lamp-lit street,
  Where waits the pillow of thy breast and thee.

'There shall be no night there' – no curtained pane
  To shroud love's speechlessness and loose thy hair
For kisses swift and sweet as falling rain.
  No soft release of life – no evening prayer.
  Nor shall we waking greet the dawn, aware
That with the darkness we may sleep again.

V.R.I.

I. January 22nd, 1901

'A Nation's Sorrow.' No. In that strange hour
  We did but note the flagging pulse of day,
  The sudden pause of Time, and turn away
Incredulous of grief; beyond the power
Of question or of tears. Thy people's pain
  Was their perplexity: Thou could'st not be
God's and not England's. Let Thy spirit reign,
  For England is not England without Thee.
Still Thine, Immortal Dead, she still shall stake
  Thy fame against the world, and hold supreme
Thy unsuspended sway. Then lay not down
  Thy sceptre, lest her Empire prove a dream
Of Thine, great, gentle Sleeper, who shalt wake
  When God doth please, to claim another crown.

II. February 2nd, 1901

When, wrapped in the calm majesty of sleep,
  She passes through her people to her rest,
  Has she no smile in slumber? Is her breast,
Even to their sorrow, pulseless? Shall they weep
And She not with them? Nothing is so strange
  As this, that England's passion, be it pain,
  Or joy, or triumph, never shall again
Find voice in her. No change is like this change.
For all this mute indifference of death,
  More dear She is than She has ever been.
  The dark crowd gathers: not 'The Queen! The Queen!'
Upon its lips to-day. A quickened breath –
  She passes – through the hush, the straining gaze,
  The vast, sweet silence of its love and praise.

To a Little Child in Death

Dear, if little feet make little journeys,
    Thine should not be far;
        Though beyond the faintest star,
        Past earth's last bar,
        Where angels are,
            Thou hast to travel –
Cross the far blue spaces of the sea,
Climb above the tallest tree,
Higher up than many mountains be;
    Sure there is some shorter way for thee,
Since little feet make little journeys.

Then, if smallest limbs are soonest weary,
    Thou should'st soon be there;
        Stumbling up the golden stair,
        Where the angels' shining hair

Brushes dust from baby faces.
Very, very gently cling
To a silver-edged wing,
And peep from under.
Then thou'lt see the King,
Then will many voices sing,
And thou wilt wonder.
Wait a little while
For Him to smile,
Who calleth thee.
He who calleth all,
Both great and small,
From over mountain, star and sea,
Doth call the smallest soonest to His knee,
Since smallest limbs are soonest weary.

Péri en mer

(CAMARET)

One day the friends who stand about my bed
Will slowly turn from it to speak of me
Indulgently, as of the newly dead,
Not knowing how I perished by the sea,
That night in summer when the gulls topped white
The crowded masts cut black against a sky
Of fading rose – where suddenly the light
Of Youth went out, and I, no longer I,
Climbed home, the homeless ghost I was to be.
Yet as I passed, they sped me up the heights –
Old seamen round the door of the Abrí
De la Tempête. Even on quiet nights
So may some ship go down with all her lights
Beyond the sight of watchers on the quay!

Elinor

My sister and I were orphans and without kin. Our mother I never knew and my father I remember only faintly as stern and chill, a dread and shadowy figure moving across my childhood – a kind of visible witness to the stillness of our early life.

He died within a week of the famous victory off Trafalgar. This I remember because of my sister's saying: 'England mourns her hero – I mourn no smaller soul, although none misses him but me. You, child, never knew your father; his country scorned him, but he was great.'

After his death, the room where they had sat and studied together was never entered save by her. His books were there, ranged round the walls – a gloomy company – and as a child I thought his spirit lived there too: never at night, without a cold and clinging terror could I pass alone the door of that shut chamber. Even on summer mornings, when the birds were singing round our lonely house, it seemed to scorn their clamour and crave a quiet it could not compel.

But Elinor, as she went down in the early dawns, would always enter, to hold – I could not but believe – some strange communion with the dead. Little in life was dear to her, but that which claimed her heart was cherished with an intense and concentrated passion which found no utterance but silently possessed her soul.

She was my only teacher – as my father had been hers. From her I learned to scan the heavens and mark the courses of the stars; to reverence – above God – the earth, which was, she said, the only Deity before which man might bow. My childish eyes were dazzled with wild pictures of unknown and distant lands, peopled with savage creatures and unmolested by humanity, where nature's voice and nature's spirit might be heard and felt alone. Such scenes she chose with which to crowd my dreams; or sometimes, in the firelight, crouched beside her knee, I listened to queer goblin tales of still remoter regions, worlds which her own weird phantasy created, depicted with a marvellous and eerie power.

If ever by look or gesture I betrayed disturbance, she would pause and look with a troubled wonder into my face upturned to hers in infantine dismay. Then, taking my hand, her voice, losing the magic ring which such recitals lent it, would become compelling, while she drove determinedly away the things which most she hated – frailty and fear.

One night I vividly recall – a night of mingled rest and horror, still potent to awake sensations which have passed away.

The wind was howling round our desolate dwelling, wreathing the walls with dreary music, such as might spring from wandering forsaken spirits driven from their dark homes into a world which once they knew but now knew them no more.

I stood by the hearth of our firelit kitchen – where then we always sat – waiting for Agatha, our old and only servant, to fetch me up to bed. But she called down to me from a chamber overhead, bidding me come as it was growing late. 'Miss Jean, Miss Jean.' I heard the summons plainly and could not nerve my feet to take that solitary journey up the stair: but when my sister's voice broke in – a voice not to be disregarded – I dare not linger, so casting a wistful glance at the kind glow behind me, I crept up, shivering and fearful, planning to pass quickly and boldly my father's shut, mysterious door.

But it was open, and the moaning wind swept through. I clutched the stair-rail while my fascinated gaze was fastened on the entrance. Across the long low room beams of bright moonlight strayed. I stood before the threshold, powerless to pass it, my eyes fixed first upon the chequered floor. Travelling from thence, they were confronted by a vision – faint but awful – and I saw a figure, white and indistinct but unmistakable, stretched across my father's dimly outlined chair. A cry burst from me. I stayed, paralysed, helplessly shrieking, gazing, while the wind mingled its weary calls with my affrighted cry. A dark form suddenly sprang forth shrouding the figure in the chair, casting a shadow on the silvered floor. It came towards me and I fell half senseless – not oblivious of the horror which thrilled like a freezing current through my blood. A darkness followed; then I found myself shaking and dazed upon my sister's bed, and felt her strong, assuring hands on mine.

'What ails you, Jean?' she asked.

I told her and she listened with a sombre frown.

'The thing you saw was not your father's wraith', she said, 'only some cloth which I left in the room this morning – meaning to sew. The moonlight and your disordered fancy conjured it into shape and terror. Go down now – handle it – and see.'

Her will was stronger than my dread – her words conveyed no reassurance. I was still struck, possessed, but dare not disobey. She lifted and led me to the door, set me on the dark staircase, and I staggered down, uttering sharp, disjointed cries, feeling such throes as death cannot renew. I reached, or think I reached, the door. I knew no more. When I gained consciousness again it was past midnight, and I was in my sister's arms – a light was burning in the room. At first she soothed me with silent close caresses, but when I tasted calm, she spoke. On earth, in heaven, even in hell, she said, there dwelt no thing to merit fear. What if the spirit that I thought I saw were there – such beings, if they hovered near, came but to those they loved and not to fright us. All fearful shapes were fashioned from within and conjured by our fear. I whispered how the wind seemed full of direful voices – what were they?

'Not what you think'; she said, 'but if they were, would you not pity rather than dread their fruitless anguish? Out on the wastes tonight the leafless trees are swaying: well, if I watched them – distant in the moonlight – might I imagine them forsaken souls; but I should only long to still their wretched utterance, point them to some victorious peace. There is, my little Jean, no terror in life or death but that which lurks within the weak, unconquered soul of man. Conquer that soul and it will never mar your rest.'

I slept and woke to winter sunlight. As we went down, she took my hand and paused before the open door. We entered. 'Do you remember how we talked last night?' she asked. I said I did.

'Always remember it,' she said.

Such was my sister: and since it is her story that I tell, I need ask no indulgence for this recollection as it comes back to me.

It was a lonely life we led. Our home was situate in the midst of a wild country: no other dwelling-place stood near it, and the village lay some miles away.

We had no friends – my sister made none. I did not miss companionship; she was sufficient – all in all to me. She had one faithful and unfailing comrade – a large retriever dog called Rodney after the great commander, and this animal was dearer – nearer than any living human thing. She loved him and he understood the heart with which he had to do as I could not. Though I never doubted her affection, she appeared reticent, aloof and cold, and seemed, as I grew up, to draw from some mysterious source a life I could not share. I knew she studied, knew she thought, but what reflection filled her silent hours, what task induced her solitary vigils – that I did not know. Often at night, if I were restless, I rose and sat by my window watching the light that hers sent forth, for company; yet what, within the neighbouring room, that taper viewed, I wondered but could not divine. Sometimes it burned far on into the night; yet morning found her fresh and tranquil, with a serene though pondering brow.

When Agatha grew too old for the harder household duties, Elinor claimed them. She, too, it was who tended our scanty garden, where, in the shadow of bleak hills, few flowers would blow. She dug and planted, tending each stunted shrub, noting each puny blossom, with devoted care.

The cloud and sunshine of my sister's face, in those remembered days, painted the face of life for me.

When I was old enough to bear the long walk across the moors, Agatha begged to take me with her to the Church, where there was service once a fortnight. For my mother's sake, she urged, it was not seemly I should learn no more than heathen knew.

Elinor heard the plea; such teaching was to her poor mockery, and she disclaimed it.

'But, it was not within my power', she said to me, long afterward, 'to choose for you. All souls are free. If they make shipwreck it is upon the shifting sands of their own darkness. Many lights there are – I cannot say which you must see.'

Once, in a book of hers, I found a slip of paper covered with her cramped writing. I have it still, and shudder, as I read the lines which set so clearly forth the faith that made her earthly pilgrimage so cheerless and clothed the conflict of her death with darkness, such as few mortals know.

'Man shapes his destiny alone,' so run the characters she traced. 'No deity surveys his work. He alone sanctions his own slavery or wrests his spirit free. His only foe is weakness and his sole failure fear. His soul is bound with curious chains; they are of many fashions – finely forged – ofttimes invisible until they scar: the cruellest, pride; the subtlest, suffering, and the deadliest – that which caressing while it strangles – men call love. Surely if Satan lived, this passion were the essence of his person; so does it wreck and rend the stunted powers of mankind.'

I hoped that time would bring her gentler musings, and wondered – not I hope presumptuously – how He regarded her – that unknown Master – whose ministry she would not own. And in the winter evenings, or summer twilight, when Agatha used to make me sit beside her and read aloud stray portions of the Book that was, she said, my father's enemy – my mother's joy, I used to watch if Elinor were listening. She sat always in the long window-seat, with Rodney by her side, quietly stroking him – knitting sometimes – his head against her knee, but never heeding the sacred words, which seemed to me too great and wonderful for any mortal to pass by.

I looked eagerly forward to those alternate Sabbaths, when the monotony of life was broken. The faces pleased me and the singing; and the stir and strangeness of the droning hours were dear to me.

When I was seventeen the Rector died. He was a frail old man, who looked as if for years he had been sleeping, forgetful of his yawning grave. Despite his reverend air and famous scholarship, he was but seldom sober, and indeed they said it was in some unholy revel that he died.

He was succeeded by a Mr Perceval, who came quite young from London to the living: a fine and handsome gentleman, and rode, they said, straighter to hounds than any in the country. Not many Sundays after his arrival, we encountered in the porch. He bowed, and asked my name and dwelling, and must come, he declared, to see us in our lonely home. He rode up often, after that, but made no way with Elinor. She listened civilly enough to his stories of the great men and painted ladies of the Court – with which he was well acquainted – but they wearied her, delighting me. It seemed incredible, I thought, that anyone could take aught but pleasure in his gay company; yet, for what reason I did not know, at length my sister drove him from our door.

One evening they had a contentious interview which ended in his banishment. As he went out, I heard him say: 'Yet you have my sympathy with wild and wayward creatures – and they pair.'

'Yes, with their kind', she said, and added – I thought harshly, 'Here, you have no licence, and you know well enough that poachers' lives are worth wellnigh as little as those of the rabbits they would snare.'

'Must I mistake you for a woman?' he questioned in a curious tone, which I had never heard him use before.

'For what you will,' she said and shut the door.

I heard him ride away and she came in.

'Are you quite happy, Jean?' she asked, 'here in your lonely home with me?' A little wonderingly, I said I was. 'Well', she declared, 'I've quarrelled with your gallant parson. He will come here no more.' I could not forbear a sigh; he had brought some brightness into dull days. I missed him; but she was wise, I knew, and also that her will was law.

The days were darker for his absence and it was winter-time – the dullest of the year. On Sundays, I caught now and then a glance from the high pulpit which somehow made me miss him more. There was no chance of speech with him, for Agatha had long since ceased to tramp the weary miles with me. Now Elinor bore me company, saying the moors were lonely and she would wait outside under the yew for me. And she was always there.

It must have been about a month after Mr Perceval's departure, that the thing happened which was to turn strangely enough, the current of our lives. It had been a day of storm; the rain all day beating against the creaking casements: the windows rattled and the driving wind which, moaning, rose at dawn, grew wilder as the dark noon gloomed to night.

Elinor, whom the fiercest elements rather delighted than dismayed, had set out for her accustomed walk across the sodden moors, in Rodney's reluctant company, but returned early, driven back by the blinding mist which was obscuring the sparse landmarks that led to our lonely home. She entered the kitchen where I sat sewing, watching the firelight play across the barely carpeted brick floor and stood before me – a tall straight figure, finely alert, her face glowing and wet, her eyes – never matched for depth and fire – burning with half-darting and half-shrouded light.

'Well, you timorous little stay-at-home', she cried looking down amusedly at me, 'we've been through Wonderland, Rodney and I. No creature's visible in the wet veiled wastes – only the trees in fairy shrouds are swaying beneath the grimmest sky. The fields are marshes and the roads are streams, but the mist's magical! That rayless world outside has nothing earthly – it makes your firelight tawdry, Jean. Come out, if only to the door with me.'

I would not, saying, it was too dreary – chilling me, heart and frame.

'It nerves me, frame and heart,' she said, flinging back some strands of damp black hair, with a gesture of remembered joy. 'Well, we are spotting your tidy floor. Come Rod', she called to the draggled beast, stretched steaming before the hearth, 'we must mend our makes and manners for the little fine lady here.'

That evening she was gay – thrilled by the raging gusts that shook our dwelling; nor would she let me read, but sat listening – musing with smiling lips upon the storm. Now and again its violence hushed our voices – we stayed silenced; during such a pause, there came a knocking at the door.

Agatha, who had been nodding in her chair, unclosed her eyes and begged us pay no heed to it. God knew, she said, what desperate visitor we might admit; but Elinor went out with an assuring smile.

Above the wind which whistled through the passage, we heard a man's voice, mingled with Elinor's in a brief dialogue. Then the door opened and she came in, followed by the benighted traveller – a man of huge proportions and splendid carriage, with a countenance that fitly matched his form.

'Come to the fire', she said; 'you will be drenched and frozen.'

He bowed a graceful acknowledgement as I made way for him, protesting: 'It is not my wish to disturb you in this fashion, but' turning to Elinor – 'this lady wills it. My intrusion I fear is fruitless, she cannot direct my way.'

'No soul could point it on such a night,' she answered him. 'Across these trackless moors, you might seek till morning and be in worse plight than before. This gentleman has travelled many aimless miles', she said, 'and lost his way.'

I noticed that her glance was fixed on him; her eyes brilliantly lit, now scanned his face and person with a distant but intent regard.

'You will', she addressed him – and a note of insistence rang dominant in the simple question – 'accept our hospitality tonight and wait the favour of the morning?'

'With all my thanks, I cannot,' he replied.

'Your beast is lame', she urged, 'he may meet a worse mishap if you go further. You will scarcely reach another shelter and you can find one here.' She paused. 'I think you must,' she said.

'I thank you, but I must get on.'

She stepped forward and put a hand lightly upon his sleeve, saying: 'Be guided. Wait the morning; that is best.'

He seemed to ponder, gave her a swift straight glance and yielded with a sudden smile, which found its answer somewhere in her face.

She turned to me. 'Jean, get the lantern. You will find a shed outside', she told him; 'house the poor beast there and find us here again.'

He went protesting gratitude. As the door closed behind him, Agatha rose and tremblingly confronted Elinor, her knotted shaking hands stretched out in suppliance and fear.

'Send him away', she cried; 'there was never a man slept here since the poor master died. This is no place for him – send him away, Miss Elinor, he must not stay.'

'But I have bade him stay,' she answered quietly and took the quivering palms in hers and stroked them.

'All will be well – all shall be well,' she said. 'Jean, light a fire in my father's room.'

I started; it had not been opened since he died.

''Tis a grave,' said Agatha.

There was no time, I agreed, to make it habitable.

'If he must stay tonight, it had best be here.'

'Then he will have my room,' she decided. 'See to that.'

I went up wonderingly to straighten it: the boards and walls were bare in that apartment; beneath the window her books were piled in musty heaps upon the floor, and on the square oak table her last night's candle burned to its socket, bore witness to many wakeful hours.

My task completed, I went down to find the stranger in earnest talk with Elinor, who sat with a protecting hand upon the arm of Agatha's low chair. The hours drew on to midnight; Agatha retired to bed. I tended and left her sleeping: still the two sat on, oblivious of the clock's admonitory chime. They spoke of things I had no knowledge of – strange heresies, the thoughts, it seemed to me, of great but sorely disordered minds; of men whose names I did not know and books of clouded and mysterious fame.

My sister's attitude amazed me; she had met this gentleman but a few hours ago, and yet she discoursed to him with a brilliant freedom which I had never heard her use to any soul before.

As I entered the second time, he turned to me and asked: 'Does your young sister share these dreams – take part with you in the great work?'

I stared bewilderedly. She answered for me.

'Surely, no. She would not countenance them. This is the Book she cherishes' – handing him my mother's Bible which had lain that night unread upon the chair.

'I see, and this –' to me, fingering a piece of dropped embroidery, 'is yours. I have ventured to admire it in your absence. The ladies of the Court, which it is my luckless privilege to haunt, would envy you such excellence.'

I took some pleasure in this unmerited praise, and begged to hear of the gay and unfamiliar world he spoke of, for it had figured often in my dreams and now he brought it near. Discarding the dreary drivel of philosophy, he told, at my desire, tales of the grand and teeming city, picturing finely the sumptuous scene. I saw, as if indeed they passed before me, the wonderful ladies in gorgeous rustling garments, with delicate painted faces and coarse manners, fingering cards, exploiting beauty, dowered with all the historic vices and unchronicled virtues of their race. He painted the Regent too – open of countenance and elegant of limb – his evil habits, his levity and fickleness – his generous freaks and mean distortions, saying he was the finest 'whip' in England; as Mr Perceval had told us too.

We sat long listening thus to such stories as he, it seemed, took as much pleasure to tell as we to hear. At length, Elinor rose. We bade our guest Good-night. She showed him to her chamber, promising that he should be waked at dawn.

She shared my bed that night. I soon dispatched myself for rest, but she seemed disinclined for slumber and sat by the window which she opened to let the rain drip on her hands resting upon the sill.

'What of our visitor?' she questioned suddenly.

'He is handsomer than Mr Perceval', I said, 'and yet I like his features less. Despite their beauty they are somewhat harsh and cold.'

'Both men are human', she commented briefly; 'there the likeness ends. This Mr Somerset should have known my father. He comes too late.'

'It is a misfortune – since he pleases you', I said, 'that, unlike Mr Perceval, he lives so far away,'

'It is no matter', she affirmed decisively, 'for "unlike Mr Perceval", he will come again.'

Nor could I doubt it when she seemed so sure.

After awhile, she made ready for rest and I lay watching the thick dark hair that swept her splendid shoulders, framing a face which any man, I thought, might well return to see.

I had always known her beautiful; but till that night, I had never marked how beautiful. She seemed suddenly, to my eyes, arrayed in a physical glory, curiously resplendent and passing words to tell. As half-clad in the flickering light, she moved about, I lay regarding her confronted by a revelation of new loveliness, until she turned upon me those striking eyes, which shone like dark untroubled streams, salvation in their depths and in their distance the far off dimness of the stars. Noting my gaze, she asked directly as was her manner: 'You find me handsome, Jean?'

'Not handsome – rather beautiful; and grandly beautiful, I think.'

'Did Mr Perceval think me so?' she demanded quickly, adding amazement to my surprise.

'He said you were like a queen and should have had an empire, but that your people would have killed and canonized you afterwards. "I", he said, "should have been a rebel, and you, Miss Jean, a martyr, in that kingdom", but I did not catch his meaning.'

'I do', she said; 'he must have been in a serious mood to mystify you thus.' Then – 'Did you like him, Jean, that swaggering cleric?'

'I did,' I said.

She thought awhile and sighed.

Through the short hours of that night, I believe she did not sleep at all; I too was restless, and each time I woke it was to find her lying, still, indeed, but always mindful if I spoke. She rose in the chill darkness of the lulled morning to prepare the stranger's meal, and as the grey light crept into the room, I heard him slowly ride away.

The night had left no trace of weariness on my sister's features; rather a new, bright beauty, though from my broken slumbers I rose sick and heavy-eyed, viewing the incident of the past evening as though it were a distant dream. She went out early and we saw no more of her that day. She spent it roaming over the wet country, lit by a wintry sun, accompanied by the adoring brute who shared her wanderings; returning late, unwontedly gay, her presence breathing a hitherto unfelt perfume of youth and joyousness, the source of which I did not question, welcoming gladly any gleam cast from a spirit which had always seemed to shed too sombrely its light.

For over a month this mood prevailed. Twelve years my senior, alien in taste and thought, she had always seemed to stand aloof from me; but now some subtle influence drew her nearer. She sought me; opened a door in life that led me to the hidden playroom of her heart.

Then one morning there came a letter – a thrilling London-looking missive – which she read rapidly twice through.

'Mr Somerset has business in the North', she announced, 'and he is coming to us again.'

A fire was lit and burned three days in my father's neglected chamber ere he came.

This was the second of many visits; sometimes he stayed but a night, yet often longer, his presence striking me – despite the pleasure of it – as vaguely ominous and strange. We went long rambles, Rodney bounding along beside us, for he had made fast friends with Mr Somerset to Elinor's amusement and feigned dismay. When evening came, our guest would sit, a towering figure by the hearth, and talk as on the night of our first meeting. Now, in my hearing, they abandoned dull and learned themes for simple discourse, sometimes however slipping into graver thought.

One night, as he related how the old blind king, now grievously afflicted, paced restlessly through his apartments, strumming a bar of Handel or addressing in feeble accents some imaginary concourse of his ministers, she said: 'Poor wreck! what hinders it from sinking?' and he replied: 'The Tyrant of this ill-governed universe perhaps.'

She affirmed briefly: 'There is none such.'

'Yet', returned he, 'he plays a part sufficiently convincing in men's lives.'

'A phantom part,' she said. 'He being but the effigy man's weakness rears to shield and prop it.'

'Even the great Emperor', he ventured, 'though some say he has no faith, I think, holds in his way to God.'

For a moment she was silent – thinking; saying, as if to herself, at last: 'Can *no* man summon strength to stand alone!'

'It is your mission to persuade them,' he commented gravely, and she smiled. It must have been my fancy that falsely detected a lurking ring of mockery in his tone.

I had frequently wondered what was the work of which she had spoken at their first encounter to the stranger; but it had never been my way to question her: I could not take it now.

Napoleon was her hero, and they talked often earnestly of him. To me, he seemed – but I knew little – a ruthless and insatiate monster, half-god, half-demon, disastrously apparelled in the form of man. But she loved power for its majesty, careless whether it cursed or blessed mankind.

I used to watch them as they sat together in those pleasant hours and wonder if ever beings were more finely mated. She sat leaning backward in her favourite window-seat, a light flickering on the black panes behind her; her massive hands clasped loosely on her knee; her eyes, changing like strains of music, which only a soul can hear. Now and then as his glance met hers, it struck a splendid discord there, which hung irresolute suspended, till he released it with a troubled frown.

Remembering – by what freak of memory I know not – the words on that slip of paper which she had penned, the fact that they were lovers seemed at first incredible, but soon I found it one impossible to doubt.

Yet she was often harsher than her wont with him: his patience touched me. I knew little of this man, although I saw so much, and if I paint him as a shadowy, unsubstantial figure, with outward attributes alone discernible, it is because – as such perforce – he appeared to me. He took, in my humble judgment, a too great account of birth and worldly honour, and spoke of women with a lightness that displeased me, but Elinor did not combat, or seem to note these failings. It was enough for me that she approved him: to my eyes, they both seemed made to dwarf, in mind and stature, those who stood beside them, like beings of a loftier race. The future dazzled me. I saw her moving through it, like a queen; the grand Court ladies, stopped to mark her progress, whose morning beauties put their gaslit charms to shame.

And many brilliant scenes I pictured in those days; not keen enough to read my sister's destiny in her now faintly clouded brow. More sweetly than of old she smiled upon my waking and bade me kind Good-night.

Summer had come to us: the heather bloomed upon her hills: Elinor's garden beds were gay. One morning I entered with a handful of her favourite blossoms and she demanded: 'Well Jean, who is your nosegay for?'

'For your guest's room', I said; 'does he not come today?'

'Yes,' she assented sombrely. 'Edward Somerset comes this evening and tomorrow he goes early. You will miss your talk tonight: we have some matters to discuss alone.'

He came: they stayed together in my father's book-lined room where she had never taken him before. Passing the door with Agatha – who now retired early – I heard his voice raised as in supplication, and as I came down again, her accents ringing and sweet, speaking as, when I was a child and in distress, she used to speak to me.

The hours seemed long and wearisome as I remained below in the darkening kitchen watching the stars come slowly out and listening to the drone of voices from the room above.

It was late when they joined me and the lamp was lit. It shewed two pale and almost unfamiliar faces – his was distorted sadly, for I hardly recognized the cruel line his lips had taken under a lowering and darkened brow. After some forced and trivial talk he said Good-night and left us. Elinor remained with me.

'You have seen your last of Edward Somerset,' were her first words.

I started up, for the first time in all my life at issue with this woman whom I had never questioned or defied before.

'You have driven him away', I cried, 'as you drove Arthur Perceval. What have they done, these men, that you should chase them, suddenly and without reason from our door.'

'Yes, I have driven him away', she said immovably; 'but not like Mr Perceval; and Jean, I have something beside to tell you. That misused personage is coming back. I have recalled him. He wished to marry you, and I forbade it. He told me (the word has many meanings) that he loved you, child, and now, if you care to listen, he will tell the tale to you.'

My heart beat quickly with a curious joy, but now my sister's face checked any happy tumult – it looked drawn and old.

'And he loved you', I said, 'this man whom you have sent away?'

'He asked me, certainly, to be his wife.'

'What hinders happiness – what have you done?' I said.

'I cannot tell,' she murmured half-inaudibly, with an awful helpless gesture which appalled me.

'I had no choice. I should have known – perhaps I knew – there was, from the beginning, but one way. If there were such a God as you believe in, He and He only, could understand.'

'He made us and He guides,' I pleaded.

'If that were true, then He has guided. I was not made to yield to any tyrant – no, not even to the world's sublimest despot. If He made me, it is then He who made me so.'

'All souls were made for happiness,' was my last plea.

'Rather for victory,' was her reply.

I hazarded, 'Some victories are void, and some are vile.'

'All victories are great. We never speak of this again,' she said decisively at parting and kissed me, passing her fingers through my hair.

The morning brought my lover and new life for me; but since it is my sister's story that I tell, I pass on to its ending, leaving the record of my happier fate untold.

The summer passed. She watched it from afar: her eyes in those waning months grew distant and her serenity profound. My happiness was dear to her. She said one day: 'Knowledge means gentleness sometimes, and once, Jean – but I am pardoned – I was hard to you.'

Her light at nights burned longer and she spent many hours in my father's room. Rodney came in and kept her company, divining blindly that he was needed more than he used to be. But soon she was to lose this solace. Agatha's days were shortening, although she still hobbled about the house and sat mumbling pitifully in her chair. Her mind grew weak; she was beset by aged terrors which none but Elinor could pacify. The present vanished from her view; she talked often as if my father lived and our mother lay upstairs in the empty chamber, stiff and straightened for her grave. Elinor dare not leave the house; the poor old woman fretted and raved if she were absent, trembling at every footstep in the passage, crying the house was haunted – that the unburied dead walked there.

So all day long, they sat together, my sister begging hour after hour for the old tales, that if she remembered them, quieted her to tell. I could not bear this spectacle of living dissolution and shunned it, shuddering, though many times I tried to conquer the horror that my heart condemned. As she grew worse, she would not suffer Rodney in the room. He was a devil, she proclaimed; his eyes eating her life away. So he was banished to the garden, where his rattling chain irked her to frenzy, and when he was loosed, she moaned to hear him scratching for admittance at the door. Some weeks this lasted; then one morning I came down and found Elinor by the table, her head bent low upon her arm. My father's gun was laid beside it; the fire was unlit, and I felt chilled by the autumn dampness of the air.

She looked up as I entered, and rose and took my arm and led me to the garden, where her old comrade lay stretched out beside a little trickling pool of blood.

'Oh, Elinor!' I cried. 'You might have saved him; he would have found a refuge in the village, till – till Agatha was calmed – or dead.'

'He was mine; he would never have owned another master, and I would not have yielded him. He still is mine – he understands and pardons me,' she said.

She tended Agatha with still unwearying care, but sometimes listening to that babbling, incoherent speech, I saw her brow contract as if she suffered. Quickly enough, she found a means to check the pang.

My only mission was to read aloud, maintaining the old habit, for though to Agatha the import of the words was dead, she would at times sink back contentedly, soothed by the soft monotony of sound. And I remember how, one night, when Elinor had sat heedless, I thought, as usual and seemingly engaged in thought – as I came to the words: 'Thou hast not yet resisted unto blood', she started slightly, so that I paused to look at her, and saw her eyes turned to the open page that rested on my knee.

'Give me your Book,' she said that night, when I had closed it. 'It has some phrases that ring true.'

I held it out to her in silence, noting with quickened apprehension the change that a few months had wrought in her. Little by little she had grown thin; her carriage almost listless. I feared our mother's malady, but Elinor showed no sign of sickness – only a shrunken, pitiful front of pain.

I dreaded night, which brought to my ears her ceaseless pacings to and fro, and forced me to creep out and crouch on the forbidden threshold of her door; not daring to seek admission as Rodney would have done, and hardly daring to retreat. I dreaded morning, which made visible the havoc of that hidden struggle which I might not arrest or share.

As time wore on, those eyes became dim embers and her once vigorous tones like muffled bells rang slow; the tale of awful conflict was imprinted on her shadowless and joyless brow. Love, through my eyes, beheld this change with helpless awe.

My thought took shape in her remembered words: 'The soul is bound with many chains – the cruellest, pride, the subtlest, suffering, and the deadliest, that which – men call love.'

Her strength was failing by degrees, beneath this triple pressure.

Love came simply to me; my heart went gladly out to meet it; but she confronted it (this much at least was plain to me) with desperate revolt. I could not view that terrible rebellion against a power to which Nature has bade us yield, without a certain horror and dismay. It seemed, as I watched the wreck which this unnatural strife had made of her, savage and wild and wrong; and yet I could not judge her, since – as she had said – God made her so.

The wonder was that still those sleepless eyes found light enough to greet the morning; death seemed as surely set upon her features as upon those of the poor withered remnant of humanity whose life was ebbing tardily away. He seemed indeed to stand between them, gazing indifferently upon his double prey.

My lover brought a doctor from the village, a lank-haired, crooked-legged young man, whom however, it so pleased Elinor to harass with gentle raillery and mock discussions on his art, that he departed, shaking his head (whether at her condition or his own was dubious) like a bewildered sheep. When he had gone, she said to Mr Perceval: 'Dear and most officious and most reverend Sir, there is nothing amiss with me, but if there were, the ministrations of that poor youth would only make me by a smile the better, and there are things that would bring me a better smile.'

With spent and laboured breath to every anxious question, came the same reply: 'There is – nothing amiss with me.'

She gave no place to suffering, doing the tasks she had always done with flagging, slow persistence; rising haggard and grey at dawn to move with heavy steps about the household business, while in my room above I sat with folded hands sickened and helpless, powerless to protest or aid.

And since Agatha's fretful terrors required her presence indoors by day, at night she struggled forth into the solitary darkness, returning after midnight to her lonely room, where the light burned hour after hour, casting her pacing shadow on the wall.

Again the country rang with news of a great victory. England was written over with the name of Waterloo. To me it seemed almost an omen of my sister's ending, remembering how it was under the shadow of such tidings that my father died.

My lover brought us details of the Emperor's defeat, and Elinor read them with a frowning eagerness – a kind of pleased displeasure – for her nature found its element in strife.

She failed at last, and life ran stagnant in those splendid limbs. The hands whose touch had seemed of old like living rescue, now hung nerveless, as she sat painfully listening to the old woman's mumbled tales beside the fire. Two wrecks they were tossed on the same advancing waters, sinking grimly, waiting the final wave. No cry for harbour rose in them and no desire for home. I used to come upon them in the twilight, lashed together, Elinor clasping the poor demented creature, whispering weary comfort, as she gazed dimly into the dying fire.

'Write', said my lover, 'to this Edward Somerset: her strength is broken and if he comes she must yield to rescue now.'

I told him that I dared not.

'Yet you must', was his rejoinder, 'or are you ready, without an effort, to let her die?'

I wrote, saying: 'I want to see you.' For even then I could not speak for her. She was one for whom one might only act – and that with fear. 'My need is urgent: come immediately: do not delay.'

As if to mock this tardy summons, two days succeeding it, my sister sank to sudden weakness. She strove vainly to rise at daybreak and I found her leaning against the curtains of the bed. She bade me dress her and I obeyed, praying deliverance was near. She lay upon her bed, wandering in speech and thought, crying at times that Agatha would need her and she must go. At noon she rallied and staggered to the door, forced back by a feebleness that struck her with despair. She sat all evening by the window watching the darkening sky, repeating to herself at intervals: 'The work is done – the work is done.'

'What work?' I asked, trying to rouse her, and she pointed to a pile of MS in her cramped handwriting, which lay beside her on the window-seat, fingering the pages with loving care.

I stayed with her. Arthur kept watch with Agatha, who, in the room below, was rocking herself to and fro in feverish desolation, moaning incessantly for Elinor in quavering, distracted tones that reached my quickened hearing, but which my sister did not heed or hear. At eight o'clock, my lover called me from the passage and I went down, praying that Edward Somerset had come. Yet it was not his voice that greeted me, but Agatha's, wailing and distraught.

'I cannot quiet her', he said; 'she takes me for a demon who has spirited Elinor away.'

I spent some time trying to check her frenzy and at last she sank exhausted into a restless sleep.

'Stay here', I told him, 'and if she wakes, call me again.'

When I reached my sister's room, I saw amazedly that she was seated writing at the table, and as I entered she looked up with flushed and altered features. Her eyes were shining with a fierce, unnatural light. The hearth and room were strewn with masses of charred paper and the breeze from the window which she would have always open, was sweeping the blackened fragments about the floor. I glanced hastily at the window-seat and saw that the heap of treasured papers was no longer there.

I went and stood beside her, fearing I knew not what, and let my eyes fall on the sheet of paper which lay before her; the crooked characters upon it were still wet. Only a few disjointed phrases met my view; enough to show me that the letter was addressed to Edward Somerset, and that it held confession and recall. The agony of this enforced submission had cast a dreader shadow over her face than ever resistance had laid there.

She dropped her pen and sat, both hands pressed hard against her temples, staring before her with a bitter, burning gaze. I said nothing. I could not speak, but knelt beside her, resting my head against her arm. At the touch she rose and swayed and grasped the chair.

I got up quickly to support her, and saw a change overspread her face. It grew livid – contorted. She stretched a hand out, took the page from the table and held it towards the candle's flame. It caught, but fell half-burned from her shaking fingers. The fragment fluttered to my feet. She motioned me to reach it, with a failing, insistent gesture. I put it in her hand, but she shrank back and made a sign toward the candle. I held it to the flame and won from her lips a pitiful, exultant smile. The sheet had scarcely shrivelled when I heard a heavy step upon the stair. The door sprang open. Edward Somerset stood before us in the doorway, dressed with unusual care and splendour, as if he had stepped straight from some royal audience into this unexpected anteroom of death.

Silently he confronted us, and then his eyes sought Elinor's. She met that groping glance with one of shrinking torment; but as he strode towards her, she, calling to aid some remnant of lost vigour, spread her hands out with a swift gesture of denial and dismay.

He took no note of those rejecting palms, but captured them and covered them with close caresses, while she stood passive, dazed, until he drew her into a sudden fast embrace. But for a moment, she lay there, then with a final effort, freed herself and thrust him off. Standing erect and motionless, she pressed both hands across her eyes and lifted one fierce, ringing and revulsive cry: her voice – a spark of anguish – dropped and flickered, then burst again to living flame.

'Thou hast not yet resisted – unto blood.'

It was her final utterance.

Till dawn we watched with her.

At dawn she died.

The Minnow Fishers

'– To be calm without mental fear is the ideal of nature.'

– R.J.

It was when we lived near Maida Vale of melancholy memory: I was walking home one horribly damp afternoon by way of the canal, when suddenly out of the mist I heard a faint, rather squeaky, but quite collected exclamation. The words I did not catch; from the events which followed they seem to have been 'fetch 'im out'; but it was not repeated and I should not have noticed it but that a carpenter, who had been trudging on in front of me, pulled up and started running to the bank.

I followed, curiously, at my leisure, and arrived at the canal. Nothing more startling met my eyes than three minute and very shabby anglers, seated perilously near the edge and in a row, waiting immovably for bites.

The puff and hurry of the carpenter behind them might have been a passing breeze; they did not notice it, and for my part I couldn't make it out till he flung down his bag of tools and began dragging off his coat. Then I saw something, something like a piece of sacking floating idly on the stagnant yellow water some yards away from the three placid blobs. Just a bit of drifting stuff, but the imaginative carpenter jumped in and grabbing at it brought it eventually to the bank.

The minnow fishers, with their six small eyes fixed on three little lines, had not apparently observed the rescue, or if they had it wasn't suffered to distract them from the business in hand. I helped the carpenter to haul his burden up the bank, and from a bit of twig and twine entangled in that dripping lump I rapidly concluded that the tranquil band had previously numbered four. The rescued atom was a painful spectacle – suggestive of a crimson air-ball, a gruesome penny toy.

'Been in some time,' remarked the carpenter reflectively. 'Thing is to hold 'im upside down to let the water out. Belongs to those blank nippers over there. Hi, there!' he shouted.

The nearest two were rigid, but the farthest one, I thought, was moved to come to our assistance. A mistake; he was but bending dangerously forward, warily drawing up his line; it was tremor of false hope; he let it down again, and relapsed to patient stone.

Meanwhile we pumped and worked, how long I cannot exactly say; it seemed a most unconscionable time; the carpenter humanely blasphemous, poor chap, and dripping wet.

It seemed a hopeless job; it was decidedly exhausting; blown and gasping we kept on however. They kept on. You can't imagine anything quite so relentless and remote as they way *they* kept on, those three remorseless specks, intent, oblivious, aloof; three tiny profiles and three spindly lines as calm and obdurate as Fate. They might have stood for it; one felt at last that they were not to be disturbed; that there was something mystical, symbolic, in their complete detachment from our distant and unnecessary violence.

But at last we brought him round, a miserable object blinking palely out again on life, laboriously restored to the damp dusk, the cheerless vista of the dingy stretches of the bank, the stagnant water and impassive friends.

'Must have been in a goodish time,' the carpenter repeated, looking down on the wet bundle at his feet and slowly putting on his coat. 'Belongs to those three limbs; they'll have to rouse theirselves and take him home. Leave that to you, Mister; I must be getting on; I'm not exactly dry.' And shouldering his bag, with a polite 'Good evening to you', he walked off.

I went across and seized the first of the three fishers by the collar.

'Does this small boy belong to you?' I asked severely.

Gently, considerate of his task, he disengaged himself with a remonstrant 'Hold off, guv'nor, let us be.'

With a shade more sternness I attacked the second. He also shook me off ungraciously, but pointed to the third. 'Ask 'im,' he added on an afterthought and with an obvious sense of treachery, 'it's 'is brother.'

I proceeded to the third. On pressure, brutal and persistent, he admitted the relationship. 'Well, if 'e is, *they* brought 'im out,' indicating with a thumb the other two, who made no sign, trusting to silence and the claims of blood to rid them of annoyance.

Dislodging the reluctant and resentful relative, I gave the

tottering victim to his care and pushed them off, following distrustfully for some distance in their wake.

Before he turned to leave the bank, the injured relative bestowed on his betrayer a vindictive cuff, which met with no response. While we moved off, the two remaining minnow fishers sat serenely on.

For them Peace had resumed her reign. Silence her smile; composure wrapped them and the incident was closed.

The Wheat

'Don't let them cut the Wheat', he had said, sitting up in bed and falling back on it, his face towards the window opening on to the row of windows opposite, in the brickwork of the London street. All through his illness there had been no delirium so that this touch of it at the end seemed strange to them. 'Up to that moment he was quite himself and they were so unlike him', Amy said to her Mother repeating his words about the cutting of the wheat.

No one had known, and half the time he had hardly known himself, but lying there, taking medicines and being read to, he saw how, on and off, it had been with him ever since he was a boy, that Something behind him which he hadn't got at and that other sense of not being altogether Here.

Work took it off and he was always at it, in or out of the house, but even at the Bank, taking in cheques and handing out gold across the counter, now and then it came to him that it wasn't he who was doing it; that he was really somewhere else and that the cheques and the scales and the sovereigns were not real things. He hadn't much, but all the same he hated money – the look, the feel, the idea of it, perhaps because he stood in a bath of it (someone else's bath) all day from 10 to 4.

Fishermen now – ! They had little and kept no hours. He would have liked to be a fisherman. He had watched them, once, on a holiday, from the ferry steps, taking the boats out, hoisting sail, and tacking, sometimes from one side of the harbour to the other, an hour, two hours – getting in. And out at sea, too, out at Sea!

Or a farm hand. He would have liked to follow the plough. There was something about a furrow, the smell of the earth, the give of it under your feet, the brownness, the evenness, the everlastingness of it, up and down – which got hold of you like the sea; the smell and feel of the water, the blueness, the distance, the everlastingness of that. And then the horses – the team of the plough. He could have lived with horses all his life. Sometimes he thought he would have liked to be an animal. Take cats for instance – lying about, blinking and dozing; they had a secret worth knowing if it was only how to get all the heat and stillness and happiness out of the sun.

Those men and animals he fancied had it – the thing he hadn't got at, which was somehow in the sunshine and the night: in lights, too, lamps along the winter streets, and shadows cutting across the parapets of the bridges.

Music would bring it, the band in the Green Park on Sunday evenings; and words from anywhere, in the pages of a newspaper – words like Victory and the Shepherd's Star and the South of France. There was another too which music brought, in which for him all loveliness had once been painted and blotted out, a woman's name. Everything about her had been dreamlike and a fragrance; and at first it was as pure loveliness he saw her, not a thing to touch, simply to wonder at; but later he would lie awake not sure if he could stand it if he didn't touch it; wishing that she would come to him through the night, and show him how to touch it; it was too bewildering alone.

One day he tried to say this to her, and it was difficult: she was arranging flowers. Suddenly he looked up and found she wasn't listening and he had never wanted to speak to anyone about anything again.

And he had married Amy.

After that, as time went on, he came to have only one desire – to be alone: but with Amy you could never be alone, even when she wasn't there: he hoped some day he should get used to her as he had got used to the scales and sovereigns at the Bank.

It was a month or so before his illness that it occurred to him he must have spent his life in sleep, because all at once, things were beginning to stand out for him in a new sort of daylight, so near that however far off they were he seemed almost able to touch them, and so clearly that he might have been looking at them through a pair of field-glasses.

And then one afternoon he discovered that there were only three things on this earth: from the Bank steps, even from the house steps he found them in nearly everything except in his street and over there, on the counter, in the notes and gold.

Everywhere else – and they were in remembered things, the bronze of the seaweed against the grey of the quay-wall; the sweep of a man's hand broadcasting along the furrow: the throb in the breasts of things that ought to be flying but could hardly hold their heads up in the boxes of the bird-shops.

A little while ago he had thought there were a hundred things but now he knew there were just these three which he was beginning to get hold of, and the place where they seemed to him most to be, all together, was in the fields. In the grass, the greenness, the wave of it in the wind, and the life in every blade.

And then he was struck down.

For weeks these women had rustled about the room, pouring stuff down his throat and talking about him in whispers behind a screen; and an Angel of God could not have got them out; but what chiefly worried him was being there shut in.

He broke free, in a way, by thinking of walks in bygone holidays – before his marriage – the roads and the footpaths; and one day he asked Amy for the stick which had gone with him on which he had notched things in memory of the places, but she didn't bring it up.

The next day he asked her Mother for it who said 'Oh, I think she has given it to Tom' (Tom was Amy's brother), and after that when the Nurse came in to tell him how nicely he was getting on he laughed and took no notice of any one of them again.

He simply turned round and lay still and got over a stile into the fields and went on and on.

Sometimes it was spring there and twilight was over them; he liked that best; but this morning it was the August sunshine and they were August fields.

Fields – fields, quite endless, mile after mile of gold; they were the real gold – the wheat, stirring gently, with just above it the green, the line of the hedge and higher up, over it all the blue.

They were there, all three, the only things: the gold, the stir and the folded ear; they were in the wheat and his hand was passing over it and it was passing something into his hand.

All that there was or ever would be – he wanted to have it, to keep it: he was afraid of losing it: that was terror. It made him start up, it made him cry out almost as if he had seen them doing it – he didn't want them to cut down the wheat.

An Old Servant

As a child not much higher than her knee, I remember climbing upstairs to bed in front of her, dreading that saying which followed too often on downstairs good-nights, 'I am all behind like the cow's tail'; a wretched joke which kept one awake for hours doing sums on the knots of the counterpane to prove that she could live on for years and years and was not really so very old. She was then, in fact, about fifty, with the erect swinging gait and most wonderful eyes of youth, undimmed from the day when, a girl of twenty, she had come up from her North-country village to our grandmother's London home; in time being chosen to follow her young mistress on her marriage to the less prosperous house, with its new economies and harder duties, in which we were born.

There, twenty-six years of her life were spent between the attic nursery and the basement kitchen, standing downstairs over the fire, sitting upstairs at the round table; in cooking, washing, sewing; in planning for us small treats and great careers; patching clothes and family quarrels; in an endless learning of new tasks and the making of little jests – a life of gay and monotonous and unbroken toil.

To us as children she was as fixed a part of the universe as the bath (cruelly cold in winter) into which she plunged us every morning, and the stars to which she pointed through the high window, naming some of them, in the evening sky. She slaved, worshipped, fought for, and occasionally whipped us with a calm crescendo of 'Will you? *Will you??* WILL YOU?' between the spanks; but for all that, she was not a grown-up person. She knew everything and could do everything, and she had an odd excrescence of authority; otherwise she was one of Us. At fifty she had not outgrown the absorbing conversion of lumps of sugar into 'pig's blood' over the kitchen gas, the sheer excitement of colour in a box of chalks, or the thrill of the blare of a penny trumpet. Mr Noah of the nursery ark to her, as to us, was as real a personage, and the player caught cheating at croquet in the Square an object of the same passionate and personal dislike.

On the first of the month, when her wages were paid, a large bag of tarts was bought from a grubby little shop near Covent Garden, to which a long pilgrimage had to be made – not because the tarts there were superior; on the contrary – to put fresh heart into the seedy widow who had not made the confectionery business a success; and there was a fairing for everyone in the house except the too exalted head.

In later *blasés* years, when only for her the glamour in such small things remained, the money was put on a horse or sunk in a lottery ticket, and it was she who stood to the last on the battlements of those lordly castles, built each month in Spain, before they fell.

Throughout the year her reading was limited to the Bible (herein mainly to the Book of Proverbs) and a cheap weekly comic paper; but on Christmas Eve she flung into the festooned disorder of the nursery a pile of Christmas numbers, and thenceforth walked with us, for a week or two, in the world of pure romance. Red lights gleamed from Manor House windows; ostlers bandied jests in the courtyards of lonely inns; the crack of whips and the hoofs of post-horses drowned the wheels of the crawling cab and the bell of the muffin-man ting-tinging down our long, dull street; while we glided down broad oak staircases and swore in the halls of holly-decked mansions, where above, ghosts stalked through the corridors, and below there was always dancing, or lost ourselves on the great white road outside where the snow was always falling, in a whirl of highwaymen and elopements.

She would not read herself, and did not encourage us to read, the daily papers, packed, she declared, with bribery and money-getting and slander that were no business of ours. 'He that goeth about as a tale-bearer . . . meddle not with him', she used to say when it fell to her to place *The Times* on the breakfast table; and on politics, in her presence or domain, she would have no discussion: if on stairs or in passages she overheard it, she remarked simply, 'As for lies I hate and abhor them', and passed on.

Yet as we grew older, however much she disapproved of this or that youthful escapade, she did not openly oppose or condemn it; her ideal of service was to obey, and of judgement to wait. And when she was called upon to deliver the secret note or the unhallowed bouquet, she would stand stiff-backed and sorrowful-eyed, holding it in her strong, beautifully-shaped, rough hand, to 'receive instructions', with an impassive 'Very well, sir', which was not convincing. On the making of verses and the smoking of cigarettes, referred to as 'This smoking' and 'That poetry', she looked with impartial hatred, sweeping the ash and sheets of pathetically laboured MSS into her dust-pan with a gesture of indiscriminate disgust. Both practices, she told us, were 'injurious to the brain'. She believed in life with the passion and some of the recklessness of the youth she had never lost; but not in books. She worshipped work without understanding any which was not active or obviously productive, though of the making or keeping of money she had a deep and practical disgust, warning us constantly against the snare of riches, save those unsought and sent by the Lord, to which, she said, 'He adds no sorrow.'

The minimum wage would have had no interest for her: it was with the maximum of labour that she was passionately concerned; and her crowded round of cares and duties, which would have taxed the energies of women half her age, was never complete without some added responsibility, usually a protégé, for whom the hat went round. One winter it was 'an old body' who obstinately subsisted (I think at Penge) on some farcical sum per week, whom at acute personal inconvenience out of our own pitiful allowances we were forced to keep in coals till she considerately died; only to be at once replaced by a one-legged crossing-sweeper in the Gray's Inn Road, whose call for maintenance in comforters and camphorated oil (for the living leg) gave us for years no pause.

She came of very humble stock, and as a child had been for a year or two to a North-country dame-school; beyond this, she boasted, she had had no 'book learning' or any sort of education. But somewhere she had learned perfect manners, in speaking an unusual purity of accent, in writing a style that had the force and dignity of the Elizabethan; and, above all, a power of 'mastering', as she called it, any task to which she 'set her hand'.

She was always a beautiful woman, with the air and instincts of a great lady and the tact of a born diplomatist; and if by any twist of fate she had been called – as the phrase goes – to some high position, to this, too, reluctantly, she would have 'set her hand', for of her own calling, even to the badges of it, her caps and aprons, she was very proud. It was she who trained the long succession of raw girls from the country, sending them forth, when the inevitable time to 'better' themselves arrived, with an '*Ite, missa est*', and a bright half-sovereign in their pockets. Sullen or wild or stupid or intractable they came, and tamed and sweetened they went away. She did not insist, but she was never tired, and in the end she won. If the young persons of eighteen could not be persuaded out of bed in the bitter winter mornings, the younger woman of sixty got up an hour or two earlier to 'bustle about' over the doorstep and the detested grates, till from a sense of the mere indecency of it they rose at length betimes.

And it must be said for them that, bettered beyond recognition, and flaunting scandalous millinery, from Walmer and Bath and Talbot Square they swaggered back to report themselves to the 'Old Captain'.

A long record of wisdom and devotion and uprightness must have gone to win for her the place of chief friend and adviser and, when trouble came to the house, of consoler which she came to hold. There was nothing conscious or masterful about it; it was simply the gentle, irresistible mastery of the strongest, clothed with an old-world deference. She remained 'With duty, the humble and obedient Servant' she signed herself in rare letters (some three or four a year), in which the note was always so gay and the phrase often so stately, written with difficulty, as with age her fingers began to stiffen, in a well-formed but rambling hand.

It is natural to think of her as if she had been wholly ours; but long before any of us were born she had partly kept and nursed and stored up the shrewd, rustic counsels of a much-loved mother, then stricken with some terrible disease – years dead in our time, but scarcely for a day forgotten; and that grey remote village on the hillside, which none of us had ever seen, but all the ways of which we knew so well by hearsay, was the scene, too, of her unforgettable romance. The man had been a blacksmith – this was all we knew, and that he had made it for her a sudden question of love or duty, or of this love or that. The bedridden woman could not, at most, have lain for more than a year or so between them; they were both young, but he could not wait. It was the big rusty horse-shoe hanging over her bedroom door which gave us the idea of that device for the birthday brooch and the stamping of the Christmas notepaper; after that – though little was said about it – we began to notice the special value set on anything, even a leaflet shot through the letter-box, bearing this symbol of the young man who couldn't wait.

It was her habit, here in town, to mark the seasons by a bygone calendar: to remember, walking through the London streets in spring, the carts going along the tracks, the fresh-turned furrows, the violets and celandines of the fields. Later, the first hedge roses, bees busy in summer gardens, the autumn apple-gathering, the starved birds in winter, the stiffness to the spade and the plough of the frost-bound earth, the times of flood, the market days of the old town, the Fair on Trinity Thursday, all the cherished sayings and happenings of that northern countryside which she was never to see again.

At sixty-five she looked wistfully through the frosted window panes, regretting nothing more than that she could no longer skate and slide and snowball with the 'best of us', the spirit still keen for all adventures when the flesh, which was so small a part of her, had grown infirm.

And sixty-seven was not to be the limit of her working days; she would not be spared, and no one dared to speak to her of rest. She still dusted and darned and polished and 'contrived'. No one ever had such a passion for what she called 'contrivance', and nothing pleased her more than to be called a schemer; or if one were bent on flattery, to compare her to Napoleon, who shared quite comfortably with John Wesley and Queen Victoria the niche in her temple of Fame.

Her Place of Worship (and when she used the battered phrase it raised its head again) was a Wesleyan chapel in Great Queen Street, and this was too, I believe, her favourite place of entertainment. From Sunday to Sunday she could repeat the sermon almost word for word, and ribbon for ribbon and flower for flower record the changes in neighbours' bonnets. But there and everywhere what intensely and chiefly interested her were 'the faces', closely studied and recalled long afterwards with amazing clearness; and never, she said, at best or worst seen so plainly for what they were as in 'God's House'.

'Let me look at you', she would say very gravely to the culprit brought before her in nursery days, patiently listening to his wandering story, but judging finally from what she read in his generally swollen face.

In early years the rite and reality of daily prayers were for us strictly insisted on, and 'Forgive us our trespasses' was no idle phrase when after it, each night at bedtime, we had to specify them; nor submission to God's will, when it took the form of mumps on the very afternoon when one was going to the pantomime, an easy saying. But for herself, she once admitted later, she had never asked anything of the Almighty – 'As His Majesty, so is His Mercy', was all she cared to say about it – though there was one thing passionately desired at the end, for which she must have found it difficult not to ask.

It was her great wish to 'die in harness', and so, dropping one day suddenly between the shafts, she died.

On a piece of foolscap dated some years before, and signed 'With Love and Duty', she had set forth and portioned out among 'the family' her small possessions, to each one of us some carefully chosen thing. Her mother's eight-day clock, which stood in the corner by the kitchen door, her mother's tea-caddy with the inlaid roses, her own much-dented, shining mahogany work-box, the enamel medal inscribed 'Honour to whom Honour' presented to her by some pious monthly magazine, with a certificate for her last twenty-five years of 'domestic service and irreproachable rectitude of character' – 'countersigned by a Minister of Religion'. This document, framed in gilt, hung over her bed, and was, with the china teapot commemorating Queen Victoria's first Jubilee, of all her belongings the most highly praised.

But a few hours after the blinds were drawn in the quiet room upstairs all these and other things had been collected, packed, and removed in a four-wheeled cab, and the funeral in every detail loudly discussed and, not without some bitterness, arranged by a band of newly arrived relations; among them the plausible greasy sister-in-law who was always taking expensive medicines and borrowing railway fares, and the heavily-scented niece with the rather sunken, bold dark eyes and a willowy figure, who had once 'sat to Sant', and when not sitting to someone or other was said to be nursing an invalid gentleman at Boulogne or Worthing or Ostend. With a great display of black-bordered pocket handkerchief, they overran the house, and their moral and physical odour seemed to cling about it long after they had left it; for nearly a week they were in possession, ransacking boxes, turning out drawers, eating interminable meals, and in audible disagreement to the end about the prices and dispositions of their wreaths and crosses. I remember hoping that she couldn't see or hear them.

Within an hour of their arrival they demanded the key of what they called the 'Death-chamber', and finally claimed the exclusive right to 'follow to the grave'.

No one who knew her could think of her in either place. There was nothing there for her to do.

The China Bowl

SCENE. Living room of a fisherman's cottage in Cornwall. Door centre back opening on to beach. Window centre left next door. Door right, opening into bedroom. Fireplace R. Over the mantelpiece hangs an antique looking-glass. Beside fire-place is an old carved oak chair, on which Rachel is sitting. A chest of drawers beside centre door on which, placed on a large family Bible, is the china bowl. Table opposite fireplace. Rachel is discovered seated by the fire mending a net. David is standing by the window cutting fish for bait. He is tall and handsome, about 40. Rachel is small and slight, but not feeble, with thin grey hair – over 70.

RACHEL: Be any boats gone out today?

DAVID: What be thinking upon, Mother? 'Tis blowing half a gale – boats couldn't put out sich a day.

RACHEL *(getting up and going to the window)*: 'Tis dirty, sure.

DAVID: And yesterday 'twas comely weather and the gulls coming back down the coombe.

RACHEL: The sea be cruel hungry all times.

DAVID: Yes. Even when it do look so smiling.

RACHEL: Wasn't a sea like this that took your father. Was a quiet night, but no stars shining, I mind it well; and about half arter nine a breeze sprung up a'most as sudden as it fell. We was sitting heer when old Abe comed shouting in and called us out; and theer we saw it, close in shore, out 'pon the rocks, a girt ship like a city 'twas, with all her lights; jest like a shining lighted city, and then *(she claps her hands together)* 'twas gone!

DAVID: And when the lifeboats was got out, 'twas 'most too late?

RACHEL: They couldn't see; for all it were so still, 'twas dark as Doom, they heard 'em screaming, poor souls! but they couldn't find 'em, not till daylight. Father brought one man in, and theer was a little maid, not mor'n seven, standing 'pon the deck and waving her little arms; a girt wave washed her over to him, and he caught her, and lost her, and caught her again, and then they two went down together.

DAVID: And was washed in together.

RACHEL: And they was all laid out, the ladies in their jewels and watches and gold chains and all, up in the church theer, with the men.

DAVID: Old Abe do tell of it.

RACHEL: He and me is the only ones left that saw it and he been bird-witted ever since.

DAVID: He heard the cry of her as she went down.

RACHEL: Won't never go no further than the cross-roads now because he says he hears the voices.

DAVID: Yes, I heard him say he hears the voices on the road at night.

RACHEL: And my two boys – that were a gale up Channel. You'm the only one left me, David, the last of all my children and the best.

DAVID: Don't 'ee sit thinking on they things, Mother.

RACHEL: I do think on 'em. I be getting an old woman now, close upon eighty year, and I reckon I think more on the things that be gone and done with; 'tis the old people's way.

DAVID: Think of the children that's maybe coming. 'Tis pretty work to watch they, playing and blinching round the door.

RACHEL: Times and agen I do think of Jenefer; and of nights when the wind be blowing simmee I hear the latch click and fancy her's come home.

DAVID: Her won't come now, Mother. 'Tis over late; mor'n thirty year since her went away.

RACHEL: But if her did, you'm not the man to judge her, Davy?

DAVID: Nay.

RACHEL *(taking down sampler and reading from it)*: 'Jenefer Parris, aged 13. March, 1844.' Look at they figures, so clear as print, and the little house, marvellous like to a house, it be, and Adam and Eve a'standing, all prinked up beside it. Her done that in the winter nights, sitting heer by this same fire. 'Was a wild maid even then; but you was never a riotous lad, not like the others. A parcel o'times they was very plaguen. Father did like to hear 'em racket; he said that racketting lads make the bravest men. But I doubt it, no I doubt it. I mind 'ee, David, when 'ee was a lad, brave and quiet and different from the rest.

DAVID: 'Twould be fine and peaceful to be a lad again.

RACHEL: Will be no peace for 'ee in this house till I be out of it, poor lad! And Susannah would be finely pleased to see me carried upalong for the last time.

DAVID: Don't 'ee say that, Mother.

RACHEL: You do know it. Forty year we lived together, you and me, Davy, and I done everything for you and you for me; and now her won't so much as let me mend a shirt of your'n, or darn a sock, or set a pan on the fire for 'ee.

DAVID: 'Tis to save 'ee trouble, Mother.

RACHEL: 'Tis to make a mock of me, a grey old woman eating your bread and sitting lazy with folded hands that was always fain to do for 'ee. 'Tis to break me, Davy. If so be as her could her would blind me so as I couldn't see thee and deafen me so as I couldn't hear 'ee, and stop my heart so as it couldn't beat for 'ee. Her wants to have 'ee for herself alone.

DAVID: 'Tisn't so bad as that. And 'twill pass surely; maybe when the little one comes her'll be different. I do hope it. Love be a powerful strange thing, and strong as death, so the Book do say.

RACHEL: And jealousy, that be cruel as the grave. If I could fend for myself, and go –

DAVID: No, Mother, this be your home so well as mine; most all of the things in it be your'n. 'Tis the house that Father bought 'ee home to and where all on us was born. All your life you haven't looked out to sea from no other windy than this heer, nor gone out and in by no other door. 'Twouldn't be rightly home to 'ee elsewhere.

RACHEL: Not without you, Davy. You'm all that's left.

(He crosses the room and stands looking down at her beside the fire. She drops the net and takes his hand.)

You've always been brave and good to me.

DAVID: And you to me.

(Enter Susannah, a tall, red-haired, very handsome woman of twenty-three, a beautiful primitive rather savage creature. She

is carrying a parcel which she puts down on the table and proceeds to unpack.)

DAVID: What have 'ee got theer?

SUSANNAH: A picture.

DAVID: A pretty one?

SUSANNAH: Yes, sure. 'Tis my portrait. And I giv'd six and ninepence for the frame. Ziah Mitchell down to the shop wanted me to give eight shilling for it, but I wouldn't. 'I'll keep my eight shilling and you can keep the picture', I told her; so her stood out and I stood out, for three weeks and more, but I've agot it now, at the price I said.

DAVID: What did her say?

SUSANNAH: Her said 'If 'ee had waited another week 'ee could have had it for nothing, because I couldn't have put with a face like that theer staring at me another Sunday.' 'Happen you never look in the glass?' I asked her. 'Why for?' she said. 'Because if 'ee do', I said, 'I reckon you could put up with anything.'

DAVID: Her's as God made her, poor soul!

SUSANNAH *(comes in)*: The spiteful toad! *(She hands the picture, a portrait of herself, to David)* What do 'ee think of it?

DAVID: 'Tis a terrible fine frame.

SUSANNAH: You'd ought to like the face in it. 'Tis what they calls a study. Miss Maxwell done it for a picture her calls Dalilah, though her do say there were never a Dalilah painted with thicky skin and hair.

DAVID *(taking it and looking at it carefully; all his movements are slow and ponderous)*: 'Tis like 'ee and 'tisn't like 'ee. The face be you'm but the look behind it be mighty strange. I suppose 'twouldn't be properly a picture if 'twas too similar to life.

SUSANNAH: Simmin' to me, 'tis similar to life.

DAVID: Couldn't her call it something else? Dalilah baint a pleasin' name to go by.

SUSANNAH: And why?

DAVID: Her weren't a pleasin' maid.

SUSANNAH: I thought her was. Happen Miss Maxwell will change it, 'twouldn't hurt the picture.

DAVID: And will 'ee look like that in the other picture?

SUSANNAH: Yes, sure, but bigger and more upstanding, and theer be a man in it. *(She crosses the room and takes down Jenefer's sampler from its nail and places it on the table, looking rather doubtfully at David.)* I be going to fix it heer. Give it to me.

DAVID *(mildly)*: May so we'll find another place.

SUSANNAH: I'm minded to put it theer. 'Tis the place I've settled for it. Miss Maxwell said this were the only light to show it up and theer I mean for it to go.

DAVID *(still mildly but firmly)*: I'm not wishful to cross 'ee, Susannah, but *(pointing to the sampler)* this piece of work has been theer a matter of nigh upon fifty year and us would miss it if 'twas shifted; it must bide.

SUSANNAH *(her eyes flashing)*: 'Tis a pretty thing to be so set on! Should have thought 'ee wanted nothing to mind 'ee of her that done it. I tell 'ee straight I never could bide it about the place. Be you so set upon calling everyone to mind your sister and her shame?

DAVID: Was but a child when 'twere adone, and if God do please her's but a child again. So us do think of her.

SUSANNAH *(scornfully)*: You was brought up a good Methody, David; did they teach 'ee to make so light of sin?

DAVID: They teached me to make something of forgiveness.

SUSANNAH: Mayst leave that to the Almighty.

DAVID: Not if the Almighty have a'left it to me.

SUSANNAH: You'm powerful friendly with the Almighty all on a sudden.

DAVID: That's but silly talk.

SUSANNAH: Thank 'ee for telling me that I talk silly. And if I do, I be only follering your blessed Bible and answering foolishness to them that speaks it.

DAVID: Theer's other words in it than as that.

SUSANNAH: If 'ee will have it, the naked truth is that I've got no patience with the precious holy Book, wheer 'tis only all they loose and sinful and wasteful women that's made so much on, they with five husbands and seven devils and more lovers than they can count; and we told we baint to cast the stone!

DAVID: Read better than that, Susannah.

SUSANNAH: I read what's wrote; and so far as I can see if the world baint to be littered up with 'em and Sabbath school prizes for the wickedest, 'tis for me that have lived clean and honest and walked the other road to take and cast it.

RACHEL *(getting up)*: And if 'ee do, 'twill throw itself back against 'ee sure; maybe someday to strike a child of your'n with eyes so bright and clear as your'n and the same shining hair.

SUSANNAH: Like enough, if there's evil blood in the poor babe. It won't be mine.

DAVID: What's took 'ee, Susannah?

SUSANNAH *(reaching out for the picture which David holds)*: Give it it to me.

DAVID: You'm not to hang it theer.

SUSANNAH: And why?

DAVID: Because Mother'll look to see where it have always been.

SUSANNAH *(turning upon him suddenly, her face ablaze)*: Be this my house or her'n?

DAVID *(wincing and passing a hand clumsily across his eyes as if to shut out the disturbing vision of her. He flinches before her but at last says firmly)*: It be mine, and I be master in it.

SUSANNAH: Who be mistress?

(Rachel goes toward the table where the sampler has been placed, takes it and looking at it, moves with it towards the bedroom door.)

DAVID *(to Rachel)*: You can bring it back.

RACHEL *(quietly and unresentfully)*: I would sooner take it away. *(Rachel goes in with it to the bedroom, closing the door behind her. Susannah and David face each other, David grave, Susannah at first defiant but suddenly melting she goes towards him, touches his arm and looks down at him with dangerous sweetness.)*

SUSANNAH: Why did 'ee wed me, David, if 'ee meant to make me only half a wife? There was lads and many that would have had me, and turned their kin to doors for me.

DAVID: I do know it.

SUSANNAH *(sitting on the arm of his chair, carressingly)*: Will 'ee give me the place that's mine, or will 'ee put another woman in it?

DAVID: I never done that.

SUSANNAH: Think of this minute past, and which did 'ee put first?

DAVID: Reckon I'm new to the ways of women, twist and twine this way and that, I can't catch hold on 'em. I be only a dull slow man, Susannah.

SUSANNAH: You was finely hurried to have me, David, and if so be as I don't please 'ee after all, why didn't 'ee take more time to look around the maid you was so mazed to wed?

DAVID: Simme women do take some looking round. 'Tis like this heer: now 'tis ice and next 'tis fire, and then 'tis up and oft like a gale to sea. There was a time when I wouldn't have nought to say to things like they. They tried to get me but I wouldn't. You have agot me, and that's all about it now.

SUSANNAH *(smiling)*: Maids be so slippery as fish, so they do say, and yet the men be catched by 'em.

DAVID: Clean off.

SUSANNAH: Do 'ee think 'ee have got me?

DAVID: I be main loth to doubt it.

SUSANNAH: What would 'ee have felt like if I'd said 'No'?

DAVID: 'Most like a boat with a split keel, tossing out yonder in the dark. 'Twould have been the end of day-light, simming to me.

SUSANNAH: You was terribly set on me.

DAVID: A man most is terribly set upon his life when he is like to lose it.

SUSANNAH: 'Tis bad work when it do come to that.

DAVID: 'Tis bad work sure, when a man be past his prime and the maid in flower and all the young lads clamouring to her, 'Will 'ee have me?' and me with all my mouth-speech gone.

SUSANNAH: You never had much of it to lose.

DAVID: I never wanted it afore.

SUSANNAH: And now you can use it fine and loud against me.

DAVID: I never done that.

SUSANNAH: Not when you hurted me as you done this same minute over the picture theer?

DAVID: You hurted me.

(Susannah crosses the room to a cupboard and takes a cloth out, spreads it on the table and then stands looking at him.)

SUSANNAH: I got a devil, David.

DAVID: We all got devils. I seen a many and all sorts, and terrible bad ones, in my time. I seen 'em standing beside quiet men, on dark nights out to sea. I seen 'em in 'most every pretty woman's eyes, but that be natural. The woman was the first to make friends with He.

SUSANNAH: 'Twas a He anyways.

DAVID: Theer be nothing for to show that the serpent weren't a female serpent.

SUSANNAH: If her had a'been, her'd have given the apple to Adam and not to Eve.

DAVID: 'Tisn't right to make game of they things, but if we got devils we'd ought to quieten and bind 'em down, not loose 'em to go prancing round like the show horses at a fair.

SUSANNAH: You could bind and cast out mine if 'ee a mind to, you'm the Lord God and all to me. If I did know that 'ee loved me first and last and put no one afore me or beside me, and I was the only woman in the world for 'ee.

DAVID: You'm young, my dear, and you got no patience; 'tisn't over long to wait.

SUSANNAH: I've no patience with your patience. You'd sit patient like a stuffed bird on the chimney piece, waiting for someone to take 'ee down and dust 'ee, and never moving till the day of Doom.

DAVID: If 'ee'd knowed trouble and loss, like Mother.

SUSANNAH *(passionately)*: 'Tis trouble enough to love 'ee as I love 'ee. *(recovering herself)* And I could have had more than one handsome lad. I never told 'ee afore, but I could have had the curate, up to Gorran.

DAVID: Poor silly calf.

SUSANNAH: So he be, but he'd have made a lady of me, and put the wedding in the Parish Magazine and all; and he won't have no one else.

DAVID: Us'll see that come theer's a maid that will have he.

SUSANNAH: But I loved 'ee, David. I love 'ee more than the dying Christ and all the Gods theer be. I love the mark of your girt wet boots on the stones, and the nets when you be drying 'em, and your shadow on the wall. And times when you'm out of nights and the wind be raving and the waves breaking thunderous in to shore, my heart stops beating and I get up out of bed and go to the windy and call out to 'ee over the black water.

DAVID: I've heard 'ee sure.

SUSANNAH: No, David, you'm one of they that don't hear nothing, nor see nothing. Men be like that. But I've stood theer by the windy till I were mazed and froze, and all the world did melt away like as if theer was not one in it but you and me, and theer was no more boats and no more houses and no more lights and no voices and no faces, only your face so white and strange out theer in the black raging night. I've thought I've lost 'ee.

DAVID: Poor maid. Why didn't 'ee mind they words on the stone of the girt grave up yonder in the Churchyard. 'He came, He drew me out of many waters'?

SUSANNAH: But He drawed them dead and drowned. They was all dead swollen men and women, dressed up so fine in silks and jewels, and talking and laughing as they went down. And that were a quiet night.

DAVID: Should have had the little bleating parson. Won't drown hisself in nothing deeper than cups of tea.

SUSANNAH *(going over to behind his chair and kissing the top of his head)*: Should I? *(He gets up and kisses her.)* Will 'ee give me the place that's mine?

DAVID: What do 'ee want? To fix the picture?

SUSANNAH: Yes, and to do whatever else I have a mind to in the home you've brought me to.

DAVID: Do what 'ee please, my dear, and don't 'ee think of they whist things no more. 'Tis late for we to be sweethearting thicky way, more than four months wed.

SUSANNAH: If I can put up with it – *(She pushes him away smiling)* Theer, go out and cleanse thyself, I be going to set the tea.

(David goes out. Susannah fills and puts the kettle on the fire. Rachel enters from bedroom, with a shawl on, takes a jug from the cupboard.)

SUSANNAH *(inoffensively)*: Where be going?

RACHEL: To fetch some milk.

SUSANNAH: I've got enough.

RACHEL: Will want some more if boats go out tonight.

SUSANNAH: They won't go out.

RACHEL: If the wind drops.

SUSANNAH: It won't drop. Hark 'ee to it. And you'll sleep through it.

RACHEL: I lain awake so many nights, I do sleep now. And Davy's home.

SUSANNAH: For all the fuss that's made of David, you'd think he was different from other men. But at the root they be all the same.

RACHEL: I always thought him different. Why did 'ee choose him then, when 'ee might have had a younger lad, if all do seem the same to 'ee?

SUSANNAH: I suppose in a score of pilchers, some be bigger and better than the rest.

RACHEL: Sure enough; he is a better man, he were a better lad. None of the other lads was like him.

SUSANNAH *(sharply)*: He might so well be a saint in a painted windy to hear 'ee talk, but he be just a man, and at the root they be all the same.

RACHEL: Not to me, Susannah. He be my son.

SUSANNAH: And he be my husband.

RACHEL: 'Tis the Lord's will that every woman's son will come to be another woman's care, but once He have a'given her a son, even the Almighty can't take him away.

SUSANNAH *(bitterly)*: And a wife be different?

RACHEL: If so be as you have a son, Susannah, maybe you'll come to see it.

SUSANNAH *(deliberately but without violence)*: I see fine that there can't be two women in a man's house and in his life and he to shift see-saw up and down, first with one and then the other, without there be trouble for them all. Come soon or late, he'll have to choose atween the two.

RACHEL *(gently)*: 'Tisn't sense for to put it that way.

SUSANNAH: 'Tis the way I put it.

(Rachel takes up the jug and goes out. Susannah takes up the portrait from a chair, looks at it, then goes to the glass over the mantelpiece, looks at herself and arranges her hair, and finally hangs the picture in the place of the sampler. Enter Miss Maxwell, a well-dressed woman, about thirty, with a good deal of manner. She shakes hands affably with Susannah.)

MISS MAXWELL: You're looking charming.

SUSANNAH: I can't help that.

MISS MAXWELL *(seeing picture)*: So you've hung it there! The very place for it – how nice of you to put my poor little sketch in the placc of honour! Did I suggest it? Then it was because I thought you *ought* to have the place of honour. Really, it looks rather well.

SUSANNAH: David says 'tisn't like me. But he says 'twouldn't be properly a picture if 'twas too similar to life.

MISS MAXWELL: There's something in that. There's the artist's temperament, of course.

SUSANNAH: What be that? The part of the picture that isn't like?

MISS MAXWELL: Oh, well, it's just what I see and other people don't. But you know I'm coming down in the spring with the big picture on purpose for you to sit; and that's going to be an immense success. Everyone who has seen the sketch is asking me who Dalilah is. But I keep it a secret, or Tregarveth would be besieged by people – tiresome young men in knickerbockers – bringing down canvases to take you away on, and then what would your husband say?

SUSANNAH: He's out to the fishing most days. And he's nought but a girt sleepy child. He wouldn't notice nothing. The men do see what the women want 'em to.

MISS MAXWELL: I wish they did.

SUSANNAH: Don't they to London?

MISS MAXWELL: Not always.

SUSANNAH: Then you don't take the proper way with them.

MISS MAXWELL: We take all sorts of ways.

SUSANNAH: There bain't but one. If they're very plaguen a kiss will always finish 'em.

MISS MAXWELL: But you know a great many London women as you call them, have given up kissing.

SUSANNAH: What's wrong with it?

MISS MAXWELL: They don't believe it's the right way.

SUSANNAH: Have they found another?

MISS MAXWELL: They're looking for it.

SUSANNAH: May so well go home.

MISS MAXWELL: Oh! you belong to the Dark Ages! But you won't desert me, you won't sit to anyone else?

SUSANNAH: Why for not?

MISS MAXWELL: Well, you know, it would spoil my picture, and then I discovered you, didn't I?

SUSANNAH: I were discovered again last night.

MISS MAXWELL: No? Who?

SUSANNAH *(rapidly)*: A female-looking gentleman with long hair and a round green hat and yellow skin and a flat nose and puffed-up mouth and rabbity legs and a maid's ribbon round his neck and a white umbrella.

MISS MAXWELL: Teddy Barclay! But he can't want you, he likes ugly women.

SUSANNAH: He didn't say so; if he do, can have post-mistress with her bulged-out eyes and turned-in feet, or Vicar's wife, so like a mule in a maiden's hat.

MISS MAXWELL: What did he say?

SUSANNAH: That's telling.

MISS MAXWELL: Don't sit to him, there's a dear; he'd make a perfect fright of you. He always does.

SUSANNAH: That's what he said you would.

MISS MAXWELL: How nice of him! And so he's caught you? Teddy!

SUSANNAH: I couldn't sit to a popinjay like he, no more than I could sit to a boggart in a turnip field. I couldn't keep a straight face afore him. If a man's to stand staring at me and me at him for hours together, he's got to be a proper man.

MISS MAXWELL: Why didn't you tell him so?

SUSANNAH: I did.

(During this scene Miss Maxwell has been unobtrusively examining the things in the room, particularly the armchair and looking glass. She now comes to the china bowl, and inspects it carefully.)

MISS MAXWELL: Do you know, the very first time I entered this room – and what a charming room it is! I said to myself, I positively must have that delicious bowl, and I shall be really broken-hearted if I can't. I shall indeed.

SUSANNAH: I don't see nought in the old bowl.

MISS MAXWELL: No? But of course you are going to say it's a family treasure or something dreadful of that sort, and that you can't possibly part with it.

SUSANNAH: How much would 'ee say 'twas worth?

MISS MAXWELL: Oh! I don't know; I daresay it's not really valuable, only I've taken such a fancy to it, and it is, isn't it, don't you think, rather useless, and a little bit in the way? I would give ten shillings for it.

SUSANNAH: Ten shilling.

MISS MAXWELL: And that would buy you a lovely hat.

SUSANNAH: Isn't too much money in this place for hats or any sort of finery, with a teasy old woman to house and keep.

MISS MAXWELL: Oh! but you ought to have pretty things, you are such a beautiful person – aren't you?

SUSANNAH: I shouldn't buy hats with it.

MISS MAXWELL: No?

SUSANNAH: I been cooped up heer all my days like a crab in a pot, and I want to see the world.

MISS MAXWELL: That costs a good deal.

SUSANNAH: Thirteen and fivepence, theer and back.

MISS MAXWELL: ?

SUSANNAH: To Plymouth. David been theer once, but he comed back all mazed. A terrible giddy place, so they do say, six and seven people looking in to shop windys all to one time and cars running about the streets and circuses and all.

MISS MAXWELL: Of course you ought to go to Plymouth, and if you let me have the bowl –

SUSANNAH: How much did you say for it?

MISS MAXWELL: Ten shillings.

SUSANNAH: I wouldn't, and I be sure David wouldn't, part with it under twenty.

MISS MAXWELL: That's a good deal. Shall we say fifteen?

SUSANNAH: Say twenty.

MISS MAXWELL: Then it's a bargain. *(She takes out her purse and puts down the money on the table.)* There. *(She goes over to the looking glass)* That's rather a pretty glass too.

SUSANNAH: So folks say; old Steve to Gorran have got the brother of it.

MISS MAXWELL: You don't know if he wants to sell it?

SUSANNAH: I don't know that he do, but a gentleman comed down last summer and took a conceit for it and offered for to give him a girt black and gold one twice the size and new for it; he had it theer all waiting in a cart outside; and when Stevie'd looked at it he called him in, very soft and civil, and said, 'Sit 'ee down, sir,' and then he cried out to him all on a sudden to open his mouth, and he said, 'They be an old ancient yellow and mixed lot of teeth you got. I tell 'ee what, you come along right off with me to Helston and I'll have 'em drawed for 'ee and give 'ee a brave new set I got in my pocket, was my brother's, all cleaned up, with beautiful pink gums and all; a bit raspy to the roof at first, maybe, but all so like as peas and so white as milk.'

MISS MAXWELL: Oh! I don't want the glass, and the bowl's another story, isn't it? My man is outside with the pony-cart, and if you don't mind he could take it now?

SUSANNAH: I'll car' it out to him.

(Susannah takes the bowl and is going out with it when Rachel enters.)

RACHEL *(to Susannah, sternly)*: What be doing with that bowl?

MISS MAXWELL *(suavely)*: Susannah has just parted with it – to me; I admired it so much; I hope you don't mind –

RACHEL *(to Susannah)*: What's the meaning of it?

SUSANNAH *(sullenly)*: You did hear; I've parted with it and that's true.

(The two women face each other, Rachel amazed, a terrible sense

of helplessness creeping over her, trying to straighten her bent body. Susannah defiant)

RACHEL *(slowly and distinctly)*: It wasn't your'n to part with. *(Susannah laughs harshly. Rachel turns towards Miss Maxwell with quiet dignity.)* The bowl be mine, and my dead husband brought it back to me from foreign lands the year that us was wed. 'Twas used to christen my first child, the one that died almost so soon as he seen the light. It have a'stood theer 'pon the Book nigh upon sixty year; and I would so soon part with my right hand. What have 'ee got to say?

SUSANNAH: 'Tis I, not she, as have a'got the saying; and I say I've sold it and the price of it lies theer.

RACHEL: Wasn't it enough for 'ee to try and steal my son from me, but you must make away with a bit of a keepsake, that were mine afore ever you was born?

MISS MAXWELL: This is very distressing; I'm afraid – I see – naturally I didn't know – but of course if this is so, Susannah will release me –

SUSANNAH: I don't. *(to Rachel)* And I have David's word for it. He gived me leave to do whatever I'd a mind to in the home that's his and mine. *(To Miss Maxwell)* Call yon man – no, I'll take it out to him.

MISS MAXWELL: But really, Susannah –

SUSANNAH *(by door)*: 'Tisn't over pleasant for 'ee heer. I'll settle it, if you'll step outside.

(Miss Maxwell goes out. Susannah faces Rachel, as David enters. He looks from one to the other, sees the money on the table, and turns to Susannah.)

DAVID: Put it down.

(She hesitates but finally puts the bowl on the table.)

What's the meaning of it?

SUSANNAH *(sullenly)*: You can see.

DAVID: Take that damned money to her that it belongs to, and give back to Mother the thing that's her'n. *(Susannah does not move.)* Take it – I say.

(Rachel comes forward and puts a shaking hand upon his arm. He removes it gently.)

SUSANNAH *(savagely)*: Let your mother take it. 'Tis her work to make trouble in this house and set 'ee again me. Let her take it or let it bide, I say.

DAVID: Do as I bid 'ee.

(Susannah laughs. David steps forward and raises a threatening arm) Will 'ee do as I bid 'ee?

SUSANNAH: No.

(Rachel tries to throw herself between them, but before she can do so, David strikes Susannah, who staggers back and steadies herself against the wall. David is going out, when she stops him with a gesture.)

SUSANNAH *(almost in a whisper)*: Stay theer. You'd best take notice of 'em, for they'm the last words I've a'got to speak to 'ee. You've choosed the wrong woman, David Parris, to serve as 'ee've a served me this same minute. *(She raises her voice and ends loudly)* Hark 'ee – never will I mend or clean or do for 'ee again. Never will I hold speech with 'ee or look at 'ee, or take that hand of your'n, or lie beside 'ee so long as us do live. And never, mark 'ee, David Parris, never shall the child that's to be born, so long as I can keep it from him, hear his father's name. I cast 'ee off. You'm patient, but I'll outlast 'ee, I'll outlast 'ee; God judge atween us, David Parris, I've a'done with 'ee.

(Rachel supports herself against the mantelpiece, a shrunken form of fear. Susannah stands erect and breathless, holding the door open, and David motionless, with bowed head.)

DAVID *(brokenly)*: So be it, Susannah, so let it be.

(Susannah goes out. David sits down dazed at the table, his head in his hands.)

RACHEL *(dispassionately and straightening herself up)*: Theer be only one thing for to do. I must go, David, and her'll come back.

DAVID: Let a' be, Mother.

RACHEL: I'd oughter have gone before. And I can fend for myself fine. I baint done yet. Mother were hale and doing at eighty-one.

DAVID: Her won't come back.

RACHEL: And Sarah Yeo'll have me, sure. Her've got a tidy little room and wants looking after terrible bad, poor soul.

Was saying only the other day –

DAVID: I sim I want some looking after. When a man takes to striking women –

RACHEL: You'm roadling, man. You baint the first that has been fo'ced to show you'm master.

DAVID: If a man can't master himself, he'm a brute, I reckon, and not properly a man.

RACHEL: And they that calls out for the brute in him, what's they?

DAVID: I be all in a fog.

RACHEL *(going to cupboard and taking out teapot)*: Let it all bide a bit and have some tea.

DAVID: I couldn't touch a screed of it.

RACHEL: Then best go upalong and tell Susannah I be going to Sarah Yeo's tonight.

DAVID: I couldn't. *(He gets up heavily and moves to the door)*

RACHEL *(anxiously)*: Wheer be going then?

DAVID: To take the boat out.

RACHEL *(alarmed)*: You mustn't, lad, sea be too high for 'ee to fight it.

DAVID: I must fight something.

RACHEL *(putting a hand upon his arm)*: Don't 'ee, Davy, don't 'ee.

DAVID *(shaking her off rather roughly)*: Let 'a be, Mother. I must go. *(David goes out. Rachel goes to the window and looks out, then sits down in chair, takes up the net and lets it fall and sits staring before her. Enter Miss Maxwell. Rachel gets up.)*

MISS MAXWELL: I came back to tell you how dreadfully sorry I am for all this – this misunderstanding. I'm afraid it all comes of breaking the tenth commandment.

RACHEL: You've broke a man's heart, and turned him from his home.

MISS MAXWELL: Oh no! I hope it's not as bad as that.

RACHEL: He've struck her, and she've left him.

MISS MAXWELL: But she'll come back.

RACHEL: Susannah baint a woman to be struck.

MISS MAXWELL: I thought he was such a nice quiet man.

RACHEL: He never spoke a hard word or did a harsh act in all his days afore.

MISS MAXWELL: And over such a little thing, a piece of china! Surely –

RACHEL *(pointing to table)*: The money's theer; you can take it and the bowl too if you've a mind; I never want to look at it again.

(Miss Maxwell takes up money and is about to go, holding out her hand which Rachel ignores.)

RACHEL: Afore I was married I were in service up to the great house; maybe you know it?

MISS MAXWELL: Oh yes! I know Lord Vivian.

RACHEL: It were his father then. 'Tis a grand place, marvellous like to a palace 'tis, and crowded up with all sorts of gimcracks, books and that, and chiney and that, and pictures scores and scores on 'em all in gold frames upon the walls. But all the years that I were theer it never took me to want any of they things. I never wanted 'em. There's handsomer bowls nor this up theer, a parcel of 'em. Happen you asked his lordship to sell 'ee one of they?

MISS MAXWELL: That's different.

RACHEL: Yes, sure. This be only a poor bleak room with nothing in it to take your fancy but the old bowl, the only pretty thing we got to mind us of him that's gone and hand on to our children.

MISS MAXWELL: Of course if I'd known how you looked at it like that –

RACHEL: Why shouldn't us? To we they things is home and long quiet thoughts and all that's left of the days when us was young. To you they'm just another ornament to take and boast on and show up in your fine houses. You like old ancient things?

MISS MAXWELL: I simply love them.

RACHEL: Haven't you none of your own?

MISS MAXWELL: China? Oh yes, rather a fine collection, but I'm afraid that's the collector's vice, the more one has, you know, the more one wants, but I suppose I can't expect you quite to see our point of view.

RACHEL: 'Tis plain enough. We'm poor folk and you'm rich folk, you'm born to buy and we'm born to sell. And, so bad seasons, when times is hard and bread scarce, and us don't know nothing of the valley of 'em, you come a'poking and peering round, and out with a few shillings to cheat 'em out of we.

MISS MAXWELL: Cheat is an ugly word, Mrs Parris.

RACHEL: It's an ugly thing. Will 'ee put your hand on the Bible theer and swear you never cheated?

(A pause. Miss Maxwell walks to the window and looks out.)

It's the word that frights 'ee, not the meaning of it.

MISS MAXWELL: Possibly.

RACHEL: And you'm not alone in that. I seen many a gentleman shouting lies at the top of his voice, till he was hoarse, to catch votes for Government from they poor silly fishermen, and terrible upset when he be called a liar. And many a woman playing the harlot, with pink rosy cheeks, turn white when she be called the name.

MISS MAXWELL: The word is more horrible than the thing.

RACHEL: Is it?

MISS MAXWELL: It is, but I don't know why.

RACHEL: 'Tisn't the name things go by that'll be set down against us at the last.

MISS MAXWELL: I wonder? But about politics, you know, you're wrong; these gentlemen are simply working for you. They –

RACHEL: Don't look to me like gentlemen, they looks more like cheapjacks with long tongues and large pockets, working for their living, and soft places; and stirring up everything for more and more soft places, which first or last of us has to pay for. All us wants is to be let alone.

MISS MAXWELL: Dear Mrs Parris, I can only say how sorry and vexed I am to have caused all this trouble in your home.

RACHEL: I've no home now.

MISS MAXWELL: No, really, aren't you taking everything too seriously? I feel sure it will all come right.

RACHEL: Wish 'ee good-day.

MISS MAXWELL *(glancing through window)*: Oh! There's a boat ashore!

RACHEL: A fishing boat?

MISS MAXWELL: Yes. But it can't be a Tregarveth boat – none of them have gone out today. It must have drifted. It's breaking up there on the rocks, and oh! I'm afraid there's a man drowned.

RACHEL *(repeating dully)*: Theer's a man drowned.

MISS MAXWELL *(nervously turning away)*: You'll let me stay here a few minutes, won't you? till – I – I'd rather not see it. I shouldn't sleep –

RACHEL: Theer's a man drowned.

MISS MAXWELL: Oh! The sea's dreadful, isn't it? It gets so frightfully on my nerves sometimes. I always sleep with a night-light by the sea. *(Enter Susannah, throwing the door open violently and holding it back)*

RACHEL: Theer's a man drowned.

SUSANNAH: David.

MISS MAXWELL: Oh, Susannah!

SUSANNAH: 'Tis no business of mines. They can car' him home to his mother's, that be the place for him. I told 'em, they can car' him theer.

RACHEL *(looking beyond Susannah at the door)*: Davy!

SUSANNAH *(with slow distinctness)*: Yes, they'm bringing him along; but I didn't come to look at a dead staring man. I didn't come to claim him though he be mine, not your'n. I comed to have a last word with 'ee, Rachel Parris, and to take a last look at the woman who've killed her son. *(She advances a step and Rachel shrinks shivering back.)* Be afeared the dead'll rise to give me another blow? There is none left to strike for 'ee or speak for 'ee. You be alone with me. You'm fo'ced to hear what I be going to tell 'ee, and 'tis words to think on. Mark 'em, Rachel Parris. David do owe his death to 'ee this day. 'Twas easy work to part we, that were soon done, but 'twere the finish of him. 'Twasn't sich easy work for he to bide with 'ee. He couldn't bide. You was the one that made a brute of him, jest for a piece of painted cloam; that were the price of wife and child, for David, and 'tis to pay it he lies theer. 'Twas I that sent him to his death, so I did hear 'em tellin' as I comed along. They'm wrong. The Lord be witness that were left to thee.

(She makes as if to drag Rachel forward, but steps back suddenly from the crouching figure and points through the open door.)

SUSANNAH: Come out and look at him. Mayst take thy fill of glazing at the last of all thy sons, but never think that he comed back to 'ee. He knowed so well as I what you'd a'done for him, and if he loved 'ee once 'twas over then. 'Twas over when 'ee took the light from they blue staring eyes of his. I were the only light of 'em, times and again he telled me so, I were the light and you the darkness of his life. He minded it, I tell 'ee, night and day. His heart were gone from 'ee afore his body. He leaved 'ee wi'out a word and he comed back to me. Body and soul you had a'lost him, and if so be as the dead do rise and theer be judgment, neither in this world nor the next will he have part nor lot with thee.

(Rachel utters a moaning cry and gropes forward toward the door and falls almost at Susannah's feet. Miss Maxwell crosses and bends over her.)

MISS MAXWELL: She's dead, Susannah.

SUSANNAH *(looks down)*: She've cheated me. She've gone to him.

(She staggers forward, kneels and throws her arms across the table, with a cry of despair.)

I loved him too, I loved him too!

CURTAIN